TREE-DIMENSIONAL
LEADERSHIP

Arthur B. Hartzog, Ph.D.

ISBN 978-1-64258-592-6 (paperback)
ISBN 978-1-64258-594-0 (hardcover)
ISBN 978-1-64258-593-3 (digital)

Christian Faith Publishing, Inc.
832 Park Avenue
Meadville, PA 16335
www.christianfaithpublishing.com

Printed in the United States of America

4/22/20

To Pat Robertson —

*And he shall be like a tree planted by the rivers of water,
that bringeth forth his fruit in his season; his leaf also shall
not wither; and whatsoever he doeth shall prosper.*
—Psalms 1:3

God bless you,
Art Hertzog

Dedication

An old adage states that "We can sit in the shade today because someone planted a tree a long time ago." I have planted this tree for my granddaughter, Anna Grace Garrett. It is my hope that, long after I am gone, she will have a physical copy of this book to read and hold close to her heart as a reminder of what her Poppy was like when she was a young girl. I want her to understand my sense of humor, how I thought and expressed myself, and how I encouraged others. I want her to sense what kind of leader I was and what measures I had of Authority, Abilities, and most of all, Character. I want Anna to know that <u>she</u> exhibited Tree-Dimensional Leadership, even at a very young age.

I have watched her demonstrate Abilities in accomplished and charming ways, such as reading to her dolls, running, skipping rope and dancing – both formally in classes, and on a whim, as on the lawn at Biltmore Estate on a beautiful spring day…and when she said "I love 50's music – it makes me want to shake my hiney!"

She showed the stirrings of Authority when Gammy left us in the car telling us she was going to "run in the store for just a minute"; observing Gammy power walk across the parking lot, Anna furrowed her brow and authoritatively declared *"She's not __running__!"* Anna has always been strong-willed, even as an infant – and into her pre-teens, but thankfully (mostly) in appropriate ways! ☺

Anna's Character has always been her dominant dimension. She has shown wisdom, compassion and caring for others on numerous occasions. There was the time that friends stopped by our table at a restaurant and told us of someone who was ill. Hours later, getting ready for bed that night, Anna asked if we could pray for "that person who is sick." During a very difficult time in our lives with some family tensions, when we were getting in the car to take her home, Anna stopped us and asked if we could pray first. Once after buying a Barbie doll for her, I observed Anna lagging behind holding her doll up to the other dolls. Assuming she had second thoughts about her choice, I asked what she was doing. "I'm just letting her say goodbye to her friends," she said.

Anna, I want you to know that the happiest time of my life was when I began writing this book. At six years of age, you were living with Gammy and me for a while. Every morning was pure joy for us, with you as our first thoughts; we had adventures throughout each day; at night we snuggled and told stories and had kissing routines. For some reason I always think of the happiest single day as when we drove around the neighborhood delivering flyers for the 4th of July Boat Parade. You sang along with the radio, danced, and even drove the car! You loved swinging under the deck, bouncing on your trampoline, and riding in my lap on the lawn mower. You would laugh like a maniac, trying to steer it into the fence. You took great joy in watching *me* catch *my* first fish from our dock. You stole my heart on numerous occasions, but one of the best was when I caught you watching me intently while I was writing. When I asked if you didn't get tired of staring at me, you said "Poppy, I could stare at you forever!" And I will never forget when, riding on my shoulders, you told your grandma and me that when you grow up, you want to "live in a castle and marry a prince, like Gammy did."

My dear Anna, I do hope you marry a prince. Most of all, every time you see a tree with two trunks, I want you to think of Gammy and me. And please, every once in a while, reach out and give a great big hug to each of us. We will always love you with all our hearts!

Acknowledgments

Thanking people can be a thankless task. You always forget someone, and that negates all the good intended by naming all that you can think of. So let me begin by thanking EVERYONE who had ANYTHING to do with helping bring this book to fruition. That can include everyone I poked fun at, criticized, identified as terrible leaders, and casually mentioned either by name or category. I tried to accurately acknowledge the sources of all photographs, illustrations and quotes that were used throughout the book. They were essential to my message, and I am truly mindful of the original ideas they represent. If I erred or omitted due credit, I apologize. My acknowledgment for inspiration extends to people in restaurants, airports, malls, movie theaters, concerts, circuses, cruise ships, and on the Interstate who unknowingly provided me with ideas about leadership.

And then there are specific people who should clearly know they own a piece of this book. Certainly the team at Christian Faith Publishers has been my key to the world of authorship. My publishing specialist, Ginger Thomas, has kept me fully informed about each step. Some at CFP whose names I don't even know yet have nonetheless provided vital steps through the editing, typesetting, cover design and marketing process. I am grateful that God led me to these people.

Of course my appreciation includes those wonderful people who had positive influences on my life, from my mother Kathleen, to my grandfather Arthur B. Hightower, to my first grade teacher Mrs. Gantt, to people I worked with throughout my career who modeled *Tree-Dimensional Leadership* without even knowing it.

Fletcher D. Thompson was a dear friend who passed away recently. He was the most highly esteemed, yet humble man I have ever met. An active attorney until his death at the age of 96, Fletcher was a fellow member and former president of the Spartanburg Lions Club. As a Special Agent for the FBI in the 1960's, he was sent to Dallas to prepare the first investigative report on the Kennedy assassination. Later he was appointed Assistant Director of the FBI. Fletcher graciously agreed to review my manuscript at an early stage; I will always cherish his notes of encouragement made throughout that rough draft.

For years, my former staff members at Spartanburg Methodist College patiently endured constant references to my pending book, but they probably never believed it would ever actually make it to press. Still, they politely devoted time to review drafts and made very helpful and encouraging suggestions that I took to heart. Thank you Kim Caton, Pete Aylor, Stacey Mason, Trinia Gilliam and Teresa Ferguson!

My pastor, Rev. Dave Nichols, and Associate Minister Rev. Cameron Treece at Bethel United Methodist Church spent several weeks reviewing the final manuscript. I am grateful for their gifts of insight, encouragement and friendship.

A *Tree of Life* is often used to represent family. Mine has truly been the source of energy, inspiration and stamina that gave life to my ideas. We have endured storms that could have easily toppled less deeply-rooted kindred. For Anna's tree-themed gifts and Julie's renewed bond and encouragement; for Art Jr.'s constant love and support; and for Kaoru's embracing us and making us part of her life -- I love and appreciate each of you for all that you are. My wife Jean has been the love of my life since the moment she appeared in that drugstore door. She is my soul mate. My Dear Heart. My Destiny. She has nurtured me, cared for me, worried for me, defended me, lifted me up and grounded me when necessary. This book would never have been conceived or completed without Jean by my side.

Contents

Preface

Some 130 years ago, around 1880, Edwin A. Abbot published a rather strange book that intricately (and sometimes convincingly) describes a fictional two-dimensional world called Flatland. The inhabitants can only conceive of width and depth; therefore all objects appear to be points and lines, as one might view flat objects from the edge of a table. The narrator of the book describes his journey of discovery from Flat to Space, as the concept of three dimensions is unexpectedly revealed to him. The other Flatlanders intensely resist the possibility of any view of the world other than their familiar two dimensions. The narrator, confined for life for his blasphemy, hopes that his memoirs will somehow "stir up a race of rebels who shall refuse to be confined to limited Dimensionality." Abbott's fictional dedication of that work is as follows:

This work is Dedicated
By a Humble Native of Flatland
In the Hope that
Even as he was initiated into the Mysteries
Of THREE DIMENSIONS
Having been previously conversant
With ONLY TWO
So the Citizens of that Celestial Region
May aspire yet higher and higher
To the Secrets of FOUR FIVE OR EVEN SIX Dimensions
Thereby contributing
To the Enlargement of THE IMAGINATION
And the possible Development
Of that most rare and excellent Gift of MODESTY
Among the Superior Races
Of SOLID HUMANITY

In the world of Flatland, all objects are flat and are viewed only from their edges. To help explain the effect of this viewpoint, the reader is asked to imagine a coin lying on a table, first viewing it from above. It will appear as a circle, but as you lower your eyes to the level of the table, the coin's appearance gradually changes from circle to oval to finally a straight line. Such is the world of Flatland. All objects and inhabitants appear to each other simply as straight lines, varying only in width. The author then proceeds to describe what life is like in such a world, the road to his discovery of the three-dimensional world, and the consequences of that discovery.

In his 1983 foreword to Abbot's fascinating book, Isaac Asimov notes that "to this day, it is probably the best introduction one can find into the manner of perceiving dimensions" (p. vii). The inhabitants of Abbot's Flatland do not realize the limitations of their two-dimensional viewpoint; indeed, they are "enraged by any attempt to enforce them to transcend those limitations."

Those who practice or rely on leadership (virtually all of us) often live unwittingly in a world not unlike Flatland. In that modern Flatland, there is a focus on only one or two dimensions of leadership, with a failure to embrace the reality—and even the beauty—of all three dimensions.

Business, government, education, communities, and families

> *What is life but the angle of vision? A man is measured by the angle at which he looks at objects. (Ralph Waldo Emerson)*

need competent leaders and positive role models. The premise of this book provides a simple model for viewing and understanding leadership that can be used by anyone from high school students to the highest levels of executive responsibility. The basic model provides mental images that can be easily understood and remembered yet can be used to explain the intricacies and interactions of virtually everything related to leadership. The concepts will help leaders improve their own image and performance and can be used equally as well by anyone to evaluate, judge and choose leaders. We begin with a simple 3-D model and gradually progress through a more complex examination of leadership, finally arriving at the *Tree-Dimensional* Leadership Model in chapter 11. After reading this book you will be able to use the image of a noble tree to recall just about everything there is to know about strong leadership.

Buried within this image is a host of concepts, beginning with the three Dimensions of Leadership:

- **Authority** (Height), represented by the trunk;
- **Ability** (Width), represented by the branches (and leaves);
- **Character** (Depth), represented by the root system.

In addition, the image of a tree will help you recall information about leadership traits and characteristics, Nature versus Nurture, Positive and Negative factors, focus on Tasks versus People, and the various Perspectives of leadership. Every time you look at a tree, you will think about some component or characteristic of leadership. You will begin to think of tree sizes and shapes as representing types of leadership, and you will even begin to visualize individual leaders as special types of trees! You will be able to use this wealth of information for a variety of purposes, including the following:

- To analyze and improve your own leadership
- To analyze the quality and style of leadership in others to help you make decisions for hiring, promotions, job assignments, or who to vote for in elections
- To train others for leadership positions.

My intention, however, is to provide this information in an easy-reading yet informative and entertaining style. The book is not intended as a scholarly work based on extensive research. Most of the ideas and concepts in this work are based on common sense and my observations from forty-five years of leadership experience in higher education, the military, a public agency, and civic and religious organizations. I chose to write in the first person, while addressing the reader as "you" so that you will feel as if you are involved in a conversation as well as reading a book.

An *aphorism* is generally defined as a pithily-stated observation of a general truth. The term is well-suited for the series of quotes that you will find throughout this book superimposed over images of leaves; these *aphorisms* support points being made in the text. Leaves, of course, are usually the most visible part of a healthy tree in the peak of its season.

> *To select well among old things is almost equal to inventing new ones.*
> *(Nicolas Charles Trublet)*

> *Be patient with yourself. Self-growth is tender; it's holy ground. There's no greater investment.*
> *(Stephen R. Covey)*

You will also find a series of suggestions or thought processes to help you look deeper into the concepts being presented. These suggestions offer opportunities to analyze yourself or others and to apply the principles of the book. Paying homage to the importance of trees in my vision of leadership, I have borrowed from the science of *dendrology/xylology*—from Ancient Greek—and used the image of a cross section of tree rings (also known as a "tree cookie" or "beaver cookie") as the backdrop for these thought processes. Such cross sections are similar to CT scans or 3-dimensional X-rays used in the medical field for in-depth analysis. The illustrations are labeled *"Reading the Rings."*

Reading the Rings

As you read this book, keep your mind open to new ways of looking at yourself and others. Begin to think of Leadership as a three-dimensional concept.

I have been fascinated with gadgets as far back as I can remember, but especially with everything 3-D. In the 1950s, my friends and I spent many an afternoon sitting on the floor of one or the other of our small hometown's two drugstores reading all the comic books on the rack. Of course we hardly ever actually *bought* one. When DC Comic's first 3-D version of *Superman* came out in 1953, I was enthralled—and hooked.

About the same time, the concept of leadership grabbed my interest. I clearly remember the thrill and sense of great responsibility that came with being selected as captain of the elementary school safety patrol. A small town was a wonderful place to grow up, where I was surrounded by friends and family, and I had leadership opportunities that were just not available in a larger environment.

Over the years, I have realized that leadership is not something that is reserved just for adults, or even for the upper echelons of business, industry, or public service. Leadership *happens*, whatever the setting. You can observe toddlers exercising leadership, and some of them do it brilliantly! (This seems to be pretty strong evidence that some leadership traits are actually inborn or inherited.) On the other hand, we have all seen some of the most accomplished world leaders make spectacular fools of themselves. Throughout life, leadership by *someone* in all age groups and settings is necessary. The settings can range from day care playrooms to the highest levels of government. Families need leadership. Leaders emerge even when a group of friends spend an evening out together. We usually assume that leadership involves one leader and a group of followers. Actually leadership can involve any combination of individuals and groups. There can be one leader and one follower, or one leader and two or more followers (a group). We don't often think of *group* leadership, as with committees, boards of directors, trustees, and similar groups. Certainly such groups usually have a chair or CEO, but the group itself might still have a strong leadership role. The concepts addressed in this book can be equally applicable in any of these settings. For purposes of simplicity, however, I will normally talk about one leader and a group of followers.

There are (in my opinion at least) no special tool boxes or secret codes that ensure leadership perfection. Some leaders do have their own "toolboxes," and some just wing it. Sometimes we seek leadership, and sometimes it seeks us.

> *Leadership is like the*
> *Abominable Snowman,*
> *whose footprints are*
> *everywhere but is nowhere*
> *to be found.*
> *(Bennis and Nanus, 1992)*

In spite of thousands of scientific studies and millions of pages that have been written about leadership, I believe that the mastery of leadership remains in the sphere of daily life, and it is available to *anyone* who employs the proper balance of three simple concepts: Authority, Ability, and Character. This concept is admittedly my own humble opinion but was developed after more than forty years of formal and informal leadership education, experience and observation.

Authority, Ability, and Character are what I refer to as the three Dimensions of Leadership. I have assigned my own definitions to these dimensions (I can do that when writing my own book). In the language of dimensionality, I associate Authority with *height*, Ability with *width,* and Character with *depth.*

The Authority dimension includes those traits or attributes that define the power or influence a person possesses. Some examples include that vague sense we feel about a person who is simply authoritative by nature, the official role assigned by appointment or election, and power seized or assumed by the individual. In order that you understand the models presented in this book, I want you to begin to associate Authority with *height*—not a person's physical height, but the concept of height.

Ability refers to a person's attributes that define what he or she can do or is capable of doing. Examples range from such broad and vital traits as intelligence or mental capacity to relatively mundane skills like typing, skipping rope, and operating machinery. Other abilities important to most leadership roles are delegating tasks, time management, and public speaking. Adjust your thinking to embrace Ability as representing or being represented by *width*.

When things go wrong in your command, start searching for the reason in increasingly large circles around your own two feet.
(General Bruce Clarke)

Character is the dimension with which I have taken the most "literary license." I define the term in a very broad sense that centers on what makes a person "human." This includes a wide range of traits beginning with integrity and honesty and further includes a sense of humor, empathy, and caring for others and extends to that rather vague word "charisma." I think it is particularly appropriate to associate the dimension of Character with a person's *depth*.

Character is a strange blending of flinty strength and pliable warmth
(Robert Shaffer)

Ability may get you to the top, but only character will keep you there.
(Bits and Pieces)

The application of these three dimensions to the theory and practice of leadership is what the rest of this book is about. I want you to bear with me as we explore the fundamental concept of three dimensions in chapter 1. The ideas and examples should be entertaining, and will provide you with the tools and frame of mind to more readily accept the principles of 3-D Leadership. Subsequent chapters will increasingly lead you into a deeper understanding of leadership in three dimensions. My intention through chapter 10 is to have you thoroughly understand some essentially simple concepts and how they interact, while at the same time entertaining you, making you smile, laugh, and shake your head in agreement, thinking "Yes! Exactly! I've known people like that!" Maybe in some cases you will even learn some things that you did *not* know. This book is, however, mostly about rearranging what many people already know. Chapter 11 is the heart of the book, where I pull together all of the concepts to use images of *trees* to represent leadership in three dimensions—ergo, ***Tree-Dimensional Leadership.***

Reading the Rings

Whenever you observe a leader in action, begin to visualize the evidence and sources of that person's Authority, Abilities, and Character.

1

A Basic Explanation of Three Dimensions

A Very Brief History of the 3-D Concept

The use of 3-D technology has surged in recent years in the form of movies and television and is used in smartphones, electronic tablets, and other such devices. We can find 3-D images on baseball cards, in comic books, imbedded in credit cards—and in almost every imaginable format. "3-D" as a term or model for processes and concepts has become almost ubiquitous. Indeed, a Google search of the term "3-D Leadership" will even produce several results with widely varying interpretations. (I first conceived of a 3-D Leadership concept in the 1990s and became aware of other uses of the term only recently.) Real life is, of course, three-dimensional. From the dawn of human thought, however, many of mankind's depictions of life have been restricted to two dimensions—from cave drawings to paintings to photographs. The first stereoscopic camera that provided three-dimensional images was invented in 1847 by Scottish physicist Sir David Brewster and Parisian Jules Dubosq. Experiments with 3-D movies began in 1900, and by the early 1920s, several 3-D movies were in actual production. The first boom in 3-D entertainment came in the early 1950s in the form of movies and comic books, which used anaglyph glasses with one red and one cyan-colored lens. A revival occurred in the sixties and seventies. The modern era of three-dimensional entertainment began in 2003 when IMAX emerged, and with the development of grayish "RealD" lenses that use a complex polarization system.

Perhaps the most amazing development in 3-D technology has been that of three- dimensional printing. With relatively affordable equipment, an object designed on a computer is physically built into a working model by a printer that squirts melted plastic, glass, or even steel out of nozzles!

A Journey from One Dimension to Three

In this chapter, we will take a brief journey from one dimension to three. Through exposure to these examples and exercises, you will be better able to grasp the concepts of **3-D Leadership** (and later *Tree*-D Leadership), and have some fun along the way.

Almost everything comes from almost nothing.
(Henri Frederic Amiel)

We all know that *height, width, and depth* comprise the three dimensions. (Indeed there may be more than three, but that argument is for another time and place—no pun intended.) We may not, however, appreciate the value and complexity of each dimension. Let's begin with *height*, represented here by the line *H:*

H

In reality, a visible line has at least some width; otherwise it would be invisible. So we have to suspend some judgment and agree that the line *represents* height, and *only* height.

Webster (1960) defines *height* as "the condition of being high." Well, not much help there ... A more useful definition for our purposes is "the distance a thing rises from its base ..." We can assume that height begins at a base or single point and extends upward.

Now let's add the concept of *width*, represented by horizontal line *W:*

As with height, the visible line representing width has at least some thickness, or height, but again we will assume that the line *represents* width, and only width. A definition of width is "extent from side to side." The measure of width, then, is the distance from one side to the other.

Combining *height* and *width* creates a *two-dimensional* field, which can be represented by duplicating and connecting lines *H* and *W:*

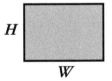

This represents the universal two-dimensional image, which for centuries was the only means for humans to depict on the walls of caves, papyrus, paper, canvas, or even photographic film, what they saw or envisioned.

Now, we open a whole new world of possibilities as we consider the third dimension, *depth*, represented by the line **D** in the figure below:

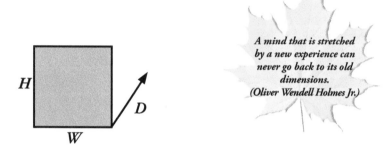

A mind that is stretched by a new experience can never go back to its old dimensions.
(Oliver Wendell Holmes Jr.)

The concept of *depth* is far more complicated than either of the other two dimensions. This fact is quite supportive of my model for 3-D Leadership, but that will be addressed later in the book. A simple definition of depth for purposes of this illustration is "a dimension taken *through* an object or body of material..." (Dictionary.com 2012, emphasis added). In the above illustration, you must imagine line **D** as protruding *back into space* from the two- dimensional plane formed by lines **H** and **W**.

Each of the three dimensions has what I call **Dimensional Properties**, or certain characteristics that help clarify the measurement and value of height, width, and depth. These properties are useful in applications of the 3-D concept to leadership that are discussed later.

I believe in people and think they are more effective when given principles rather than procedures, strategies rather than tactics, whys rather than wants.
(Harvey Golub)

Dimensional Property 1: The only measure of height, width, or depth is the distance from one point of that dimension to the other. The quality of *height* can be determined only by comparing which subjects are higher (or taller); the quality of *width* by determining which subjects are wider (or longer); and the quality of *depth* by comparing which subjects are deeper. The only quality for each dimension, then, is the measurement of that dimension.

Dimensional Property 2: There is no limit to the measurement of height, width, or depth. Each dimension can be infinite. There can be various measurements of each dimension, but there is no limit to the *potential*.

Dimensional Property 3: *Higher, wider, or deeper* is not necessarily *better.* The value of the measurement of a dimension in any given situation depends on the purpose being served. Sometimes we may desire more or less height, width, or depth. Because there are no dimensional limits, we cannot say that we desire the *most* or *least* of a dimension. We can, however, make comparisons among groups of subjects (which is the tallest line of three, for example).

Screen Aspect Ratios

Television and movie technologies use a generally accepted concept referred to as the 16:9 aspect ratio. While this can be explained in scientific and/or technical terms, I believe most of you will readily understand the following discussion without the necessity of getting extremely technical. The 16:9 ratio refers to the proportional relationship between width and height, meaning that width is sixteen units of measurement while height is nine. For instance, a screen that is sixteen inches wide would be nine inches tall. (This concept will be useful in later discussions about leadership—believe me, be patient.)

Movie screens were basically square from the earliest productions until Cinemascope came along and made screens much wider. This thrilled audiences because much more visual information could be presented on the screen, and it was just more pleasing to the eye. (The ratio was something like 2.66:1, but you don't need to know that.) Movie screen ratios have varied over the years, but they have continued to be *wider* than they are *tall*. When television sets first came out, the screens were basically square (early models had rounded or bowed edges), but screen formats settled on a 4:3 "squarish" ratio for many years. When high-definition television (or HDTV) was developed, it used a ratio of 16:9, which has since been applied to DVDs and similar entertainment formats. Today, the most common aspect ratio standard for television, computer screens and even smart phones is 16:9.

My purpose for this discussion is simply to illustrate that two-dimensional objects are more effective and pleasing to the eye in at least the general proportions of 16:9. Consider the following examples.

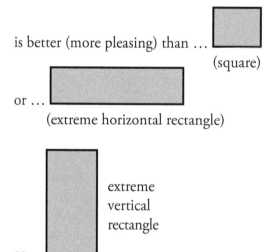

Wouldn't you agree that this shape ...

(approx. 16:9)

is better (more pleasing) than ...

(square)

or ...

(extreme horizontal rectangle)

extreme
vertical
rectangle

or ...

Again, the application of these illustrations to leadership will become evident in later discussions about 3-D (and Tree-D) Leadership. This discussion of aspect ratios leads to the next Dimensional Property:

Dimensional Property 4: Width and height are most effectively and pleasantly illustrated when width is greater than height, in a ratio of approximately 16:9.

Now let's further explore the illustration of all three dimensions. On page 14 above, we arrived at this figure to illustrate the concept of depth:

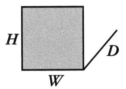

To more clearly visualize a three-dimensional object, let's add and connect some more lines representing depth:

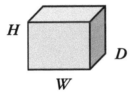

Next, let's apply **Dimensional Property 4** (dealing with aspect ratio) to this figure. In general terms, a figure with greater width than height (approximately 16:9) …

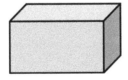

can appear more effective or pleasing than.

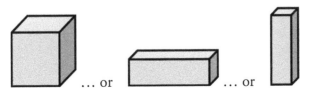

… or   … or

Applying various aspect ratios to a three-dimensional object creates the need for three more Dimensional Properties:

Dimensional Property 5: Any of the dimensions of a three-dimensional object can be changed without affecting the other dimensions.

Dimensional Property 6: Changes can be made to one, two, or all three dimensions of a three-dimensional object.

Dimensional Property 7: Variations of height, width and depth can significantly affect the appearance of a three-dimensional object.

You can't control the length of your life, but you can control the width and depth.
(Anonymous)

Reading the Rings

By now you may be thinking "What the hell does this have to do with leadership?" Trust me, it's coming soon. In the meantime, have some fun with the next chapter…

2

Some Fun Examples
of 3-D Magic

Reading a book like this should be fun as well as informative. Plus, I want to fix the 3-D concept firmly into your brain so that you will readily understand its many applications throughout the book. So let me take you on another journey from flat to three dimensions, this time with some "in-depth" examples.

Early stereoscopic photographs used two images photographed from slightly different angles so that when viewed through special lenses the impression of depth was given. A more modern device using this technique is the View-Master, which was introduced in 1962. That process would be too expensive to reproduce in this book, so you will just have to imagine (or perhaps remember, if you are old enough) what that looks like.

The 3-D effects of the 1950's utilized cardboard glasses with a red lens on the left and a blue lens on the right. The images were produced with special colors that made them appear three-dimensional through the glasses. To get the full effect of the image below and a few others in this book, I encourage you to order a pair online from such websites as Amazon – they cost as little as 6 cents each. Even without the glasses, I think you can imagine the effect, as below:

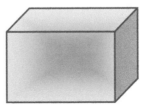

You should see a rather rudimentary 3-D effect, but hopefully you get the point. Below, I have reproduced a very interesting dual-image that emphasizes the difference between 3-D and 2-D.

www.hit.ro/stiinta-generala/technologia

You can easily see that the top image, coded for the anaglyph glasses, reflects depth, whereas the bottom image remains two-dimensional. If you are able to view the images with anaglyph glasses, I think you will agree that the image with the illusion of depth is much more interesting—more fun.

Sometimes, this type of 3-D effect works best with drawings or similar graphics, but photographs can render rather stunning effects also, as you can see in the Stonehenge image shown on the next page (www.eyetricks.com; BWH Ventures, LLC):

A 3-D photograph can provide a level of detail and perspective that is not possible from a standard two-dimensional rendering. Businesses, industry and the military have all begun to rely heavily on 3-D technology for interpretations that can be vital to their missions.

In recent years, the "RealD" system utilizes glasses that are uniformly gray; they are easier on the eyes and provide depth of field that is more realistic. The system, however, cannot be duplicated in print, so I cannot illustrate it here, but most of you by now have probably seen a 3-D movie using "RealD" technology.

While systems are on the immediate horizon that will allow advanced three-dimensional viewing without glasses on computers and other electronic gadgets, a variety of processes have been around for quite some time that provide a 3-D effect to the naked eye. One of those types is *lenticular printing,* a process using two or more images and a ridged (or lenticular) lens material. Often used for postcards and bookmarks, the process can produce spectacular three-dimensional effects. I had hoped to have a 3-D lenticular image on the cover of this book – it would have been *so cool* – but alas, it was a little too complicated for my publisher!

Holograms are used in many applications, most commonly perhaps on credit cards to make them more difficult to counterfeit.

Another example of 3-D art uses a process called random-dot stereography, which produces optical illusions commonly known as Magic Eye images. Magic Eye books were wildly popular in the 1990s and these images continue to be used primarily in posters and calendars.

The example below is a good place to start—it contains a hidden image that will appear in 3-D once you achieve the right focus. This one is fairly easy to view. I chose this example also because I have performed magic for many years, and enjoy anything magical! Experiencing these images in 3-D requires a bit of concentration and focus; some people find the technique more difficult than others. For one thing, you must find the right distance from your eyes. I suggest holding the image about ten inches away at first; you have to look beyond the normal focus point and sort of cross your eyes as you concentrate on the image. You should begin to see a little bit of 3-D and then adjust the distance and focus as necessary. It can be an "aha!" moment when the hidden image emerges!

Hidden Image

The small black and white image here illustrates the 3-D image that will emerge full-size in color within the Magic Eye image.

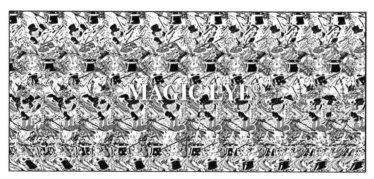

(Special thanks to www.magiceye3ds.com for use of images.)

Using the same eye focusing technique, you should find a 3-D image of a coffee cup in the center of this illustration.

Finally, you will find a mortar and pestle in the purple flowers below.

Playing around with these Magic Eye images can be entertaining, but they are also used by eye specialists for vision therapy. The focusing effort provides something like aerobic exercises for your eyes. There are even claims that use of these images can actually improve vision, relax your body, and calm your mind.

Finally (whew, you may say), a form of 3-D graphics known as "street art," "pavement drawings," or the more sophisticated-sounding "Madonnari" has become quite prevalent since the 1980s. More officially referred to as the **anamorphic** technique, this art form can actually be traced to prehistoric cave drawings. Leonardo da Vinci produced the first "modern" image *Leonardo's Eye* using this technique; Italian *madonnari* then popularized the style in the 1500s; pavement art in Britain was well-established by 1890. In the 1980s, however, a genius named Kurt Wenner began to produce "3-D pavement art" that astonished the public and started a renaissance of anamorphic art that is wildly popular today. Street art festivals are held throughout the world, producing such examples as this:

Kurt Wenner (wall-mag.com)

One of Wenner's disciples, Julian Beever, produced this jewel:

Julian Beever (designtaxi.com)

Another version of the anamorphic 3-D effect has been accomplished with simple pencil drawings:

earthporm.com

3-D pencil drawings can be quite sophisticated:

Looha Desenhos (webneel.com)

Yet another form of an anamorphic 3-D effect is accomplished by the use of distorted drawings or even sculptures that make little sense until reflected in a mirror or off a curved surface. This final example is actually a toy produced by Myrna Hoffman for the OOZ & OZ company:

Myrna Hoffman (OOZ & OZ)

I hope you have found this chapter with examples of 3-D magic to be entertaining. More importantly, however, my intention is to get your head in the right place for understanding 3-D Leadership. As a 3-D person, you need to have an open mind, be willing to look at things from all angles, let your hair down, and have a little fun from time to time.

Too many leaders have their head in the clouds or have their head in the sand. Sometimes leaders have their head in a book when it should be somewhere else (but this book is an exception); there are those who keep their nose in the air, and some have their head up their—well, you get the message!

I want you to wake up, look around and be aware of the height, width, and depth of everything and everybody around you. Where is *your* head?

The place to improve the world is first in one's own heart and head and hands, and then work outward from there.
(Robert Persig)

Reading the Rings

Now is the time to put all of this background on thinking in 3-D to leading in 3-D. Just what do you think leadership is?

In Chapter 3 we will explore ever so briefly the whole concept of leadership.

3

What Is Leadership?

An awful lot has been said about the definition of leadership. Most are honest efforts at pinning down something we can all agree on, but some definitions don't make a lot of sense—and some are contradictory. You be the judge:

Leadership is a verb, not a noun.
(Bill Gore)

Leadership is action, not position.
(Donald H. McGannon)

A leader is one who knows the way, goes the way, and shows the way.
(John C. Maxwell)

What all leaders have in common is that others recognize the value of their contribution and choose to follow them.
(Miriam E. Kragness)

Management is doing things right. Leadership is doing the right thing.
(Peter F. Drucker)

Leadership is the art of getting someone else to do something you want done because he wants to do it.
(Dwight D. Eisenhower)

A leader is a dealer in hope.
(Napoleon Bonaparte)

In order to lead, you must sometimes walk behind.
(Unknown)

A leader must often clarify rather than define a group's purpose.
(Unknown)

The first responsibility of a leader is to define reality. The last is to say thank you. In between, the leader is a servant.
(Max DePree)

Leadership is intentional influence.
(Michael McKinney)

Great leaders are almost always great simplifiers, who can cut through argument, debate, and doubt to offer a solution everybody can understand.
(Gen. Colin Powell)

A Google search for the word leadership yields over 500 million hits, and a Bing search returns 325 million. If you Google leadership books, you will find 216 million choices. You can read over two thousand published definitions of leadership. So here's the problem: the concept of leadership has *simply become too complicated* (is that an oxymoron?) for an ordinary person to understand it. My concept of 3-D Leadership (and Tree-Dimensional Leadership) is intended to provide a model that is easy to comprehend, yet comprehensive enough to encompass the whole idea of leadership. On the other hand, I suppose that no book on leadership would be complete without at least some acknowledgement of what is out there, and some interpretation of the concept. So I am going to summarize what I think are the most meaningful points, keeping the discussion as simple as possible. It is not necessary for you to memorize this information, and you will not be tested on it ☺. Just let it provide some background for your own interpretation of leadership.

Reading the Rings

Close your eyes and think of a blank screen. Now imagine on that screen everything you know about leadership. You may experience something like the snow that used to appear on old rabbit-ear TV sets. After reading this book, you should be able to visualize leadership simply as a tree—but within its image, you will be able to recall a wealth of knowledge about the intricacies and interactions of this otherwise complex concept.

From the Beginning ...

A caveman somewhere made the first use of leadership by cracking another guy over the head with a club. That was a clear exercise of Authority. Philosophers and other writers have been discussing leadership for centuries. Plato talked about the challenges a leader faces when trying to change an organization. Confucius wrote about ethical leadership, while Machiavelli took an opposite stance and earned a reputation for being devious and downright mean with his practical strategies of leadership. Current authors such as Steven Covey, Ken Blanchard, Jack Welch, Donald Trump, and hundreds of others continue to address these ancient ideas with modern applications. Increasing numbers of books and articles over the years have addressed the concept of natural born leaders while others promote nurturing theories that argue leadership can be taught and developed.

Situational Leadership

In the early 1970s, Paul Hersey and Ken Blanchard developed their Situational Leadership Theory. Their book *Management of Organizational Behavior: Utilizing Human Resources* (1977) was used as a textbook in my doctoral program at The Florida State University. Situational Leadership Theory made a profound impression on me and has remained a strong influence in my interactions with people throughout my career. Hersey and Blanchard's work has spawned numerous books and other publications and most modern leadership theories pay homage to the concept of situational leadership.

Hersey and Blanchard characterized leadership style in terms of Task Behavior and Relationship Behavior, noting that the most effective leadership style will vary with the situation. They identified four types of behavior that we can all understand: *(The labels S1, M1, etc., are as originally used by Hersey and Blanchard.)*

S1 Telling
S2 Selling
S3 Participating
S4 Delegating

Further, they described four Maturity Levels of leaders:

M1 Unable and insecure
M2 Unable but willing
M3 Capable, but unwilling
M4 Capable and willing.

Theories that Emphasize "Human Traits"

A particularly enlightening development in recent years has been the theory of emotional intelligence as applied to leadership. In 1980, Reuven Bar-on first developed the concept while researching the keys to success. When Daniel Goleman published *Emotional Intelligence: Why it can matter more than IQ* in 1995, he spawned an explosion of works applying EI to leadership. Emotional intelligence promotes the value of self-awareness, empathy, self-confidence, and self-control in effective leadership. It was an important advance in leadership theory, as it does emphasize the "humanness" and importance of values in a leader. The Emotional Intelligence concept paints with a broad brush as a way of looking at leadership in general.

Eastman (2009) addresses what he calls the ancient concept of character in his book *The Character of Leadership*. Like the emotional intelligence approach, however, Eastman's concept of character is applied to leadership in a broader and somewhat different sense than my third dimension of Character. Still, the basic premise is that effective leaders must have a commitment to the fundamental values of faith, justice, temperance, hope, wisdom, love, and courage—all humanizing traits.

The theory of *leading from behind* has gained national attention in recent years. President Obama referred to it as the basis for his approach to America's role in the Middle East. Linda Hill of the Harvard Business School began promoting this view of leadership when she read Nelson Mandela's biography in which he noted that shepherds direct flocks from behind. The idea is that some sheep will move ahead, with the others following them. This concept is used to support the theory of leading from behind as a form of servant leadership that focuses on employees, a supportive environment, and innovation. In my view, there may be limited settings and/or brief periods of time when this approach may be useful, but it is not a broadly effective technique worth adoption. In fact, shepherds will tell you that attempting to lead sheep from behind will often only scatter them in all directions. In reality, sheep can be lead in a number of ways, depending on the circumstances. The shepherd can entice them from the front with a bucket of food; they can be called with a familiar and trusted voice; if the sheep know the route, they can move without much guidance at all; sometimes several people are needed ahead, behind, and on both sides of the flock.

Leadership Styles—Getting Others to Follow

Leadership may be most appreciated and/or most visible when people seem to *need* leadership the most. When times are bad, people are most vulnerable, if you will, to being inspired and motivated by the right kind of leader at the right time.

> *A leader is one who,*
> *out of madness or*
> *goodness, volunteers to*
> *take upon himself the*
> *woe of the people.*
> *There are few men so*
> *foolish, hence the erratic*
> *quality of leadership.*
> *(John Updike)*

> *When trouble arises and*
> *things look bad, there is*
> *always one individual who*
> *perceives a solution and is*
> *willing to take command.*
> *Very often, that individual*
> *is crazy.*
> *(Dave Barry, Internet*
> *List of "Things it took*
> *me 50 years to learn")*

The Bible is replete with examples of how God chose one person to lead His people out of trouble (usually trouble they had brought upon themselves.) From Abraham to Moses to Joshua to Jesus, God always found an individual, often an apparently incapable individual, to do His work. But they were always successful in motivating the chosen people to come together, and to accomplish miraculous things!

Some scholars have proposed systems of rewards and punishments for motivating followers, while others insist that followers must be inspired through innovation and charismatic leadership. My leadership experience has included positions in the military, public service, churches and civic clubs, and higher education administration. I have experienced the pain of working under an insanely authoritative, dictatorial boss. I have been faced with the ambivalence of trying to figure out some supervisors who stayed totally out of the leadership process. Fortunately, I have also had the pure pleasure of working with some leaders who were benevolent, supportive, and authentic.

Many definitions of leadership include the concept of shepherding others into having a sense of ownership toward a common vision. This requires establishing a special kind of connection with the hearts and minds of followers and then *capturing* those hearts and minds. Members of a group must be willing to be led, and that requires trust—ideally *mutual* trust between the leader and the led.

All of us seem to know when we are in the presence of a great leader, but we may not know *why* we feel that way. John C. Maxwell, in his devotional guide *A Leader's Heart* (2010), describes why a rag-tag group of warriors led the movement to make David king over all of Israel. He says that David connected with his people because:

1. *He was relational.* He was personable and approachable.
2. *He was resourceful.* He helped his team to become all it could be and enabled it to succeed.
3. *He was rewarding.* David shared both rewards and recognition for victory.
4. *He was respectable.* Friends and foes alike respected him; people saw in David an example of good leadership *(p.18)*.

All these men of war, who could keep ranks, came to Hebron with a loyal heart, to make David king over all Israel; and all the rest of Israel were of one mind to make David king.
(1 Chronicles 12:38)

Success relies less on who leads than on the chemistry between leaders and followers. I think the business of cultivating followers boils down to this: People will follow a leader for three reasons:

- Fear—because of the leader's *Authority*
- Blind obedience—because of the leader's *Abilities*
- Respect—because of the leader's Character.

> *People don't
> care how much
> you know, until
> they know how
> much you care.*
> (Zig Ziglar)

History is replete with glaring examples of leaders who were successful through use of each of these motivators. Situations sometimes demand extreme measures, but it is my bet that most of us prefer leaders who employ the third alternative.

In my view, simple leadership certainly does not have to embody all of the great things that writers and philosophers have described or proposed. *Great* leadership, perhaps. But leadership can be bad as well as good. Some pretty terrible one-dimensional people have been leaders—even effective leaders. One might say that there are *raw* leaders—those with at least one essential trait or dimension; and *refined* leaders—those who have acquired or developed multi-dimensional traits and put them to use for the common good.

So in seven pages, I have summarized the history and all human knowledge of leadership—well, all that I think is important anyway. We have seen that the first level of leadership was quite possibly demonstrated by the exercise of Authority for basic survival. It makes sense, doesn't it, that before man's brain developed enough to learn skills and the nuances of persuasion, that simple force or power was the route to leadership?

Then, as time and evolution rolled along, people began to think and write about such things as *how* to lead. They developed Abilities that would extend their Authority—Abilities such as facing challenges, designing strategies, and teaching and nurturing leadership skills.

We have seen that the importance of ethics was recognized early on, but the concept kept facing setbacks for centuries as leaders with lots of Authority and Abilities kept dominating those who preferred playing nice. Then in more modern times, researchers and scholars began to influence the leadership landscape with such ideas as being autocratic, demonstrating concern for others, considering the situation, adhering to fundamental values, expanding awareness, exhibiting self-confidence, a return to ethical behavior, and shared vision. These more recent leadership functions are the "humanizing" side of leadership, or what I call Character.

In a broad sort of way, then, the concept of leadership has evolved from Authority to Abilities to Character. This evolution leads to my own definition of "raw" leadership as the use of *either* Authority, Abilities, or Character for *completion of a task*. "Refined" leadership would be the application of Authority, Abilities, *and* Character to the accomplishment of *group goals*. Another way to put it is in the form of a simple equation: **Authority + Ability + Character = Leadership.** This evolution of leadership is precisely the basis for the model of 3-D Leadership that we will explore in chapters 4, 5 and 6.

Up to a point a man's life is shaped by environment, heredity, and movements and changes in the world about him; then there comes a time when it lies within his grasp to shape the clay of his life into the sort of thing he wishes to be ... Everyone has it within his power to say, this I am today, that I shall be tomorrow. —
(Louis L'Amour)

Reading the Rings

Visualize condensing all that
you know about the definition
and history of leadership into
three simple concepts:

Authority, Abilities, and
Character.

It really does all fit into
that small package!

4

Authority Represented by Height

Authority Represented by Height

D arth Vader is one of the most readily recognized Authority figures in the modern era. He is a tall, imposing figure who uses "the force" to lift and move objects and to elicit "cooperation" from friends and foes alike. He has a commanding voice, a hypnotic appearance, and simply exudes an aura of Authority.

(http://dev.officialpsds.com/darth-vader-PSD50645.html)

When I decided to associate Authority with the dimension of height in my 3-D Leadership model, it was not a random thought. For one thing, height just seems to logically represent Authority. Bigger usually prevails over smaller. Tall people are generally considered, at least on initial impression, as more authoritative than shorter people. Animals, when fighting or involved in mating behavior, will raise themselves up to appear as tall as possible. One of the most imposing figures in nature is a mother grizzly standing with claws in the air, fangs bared, defending her cubs. A cobra raises its head and expands it when ready to strike. Even ants will stand on their hind legs to improve their miniscule appearance when angered.

Gravitas is a leadership term that has come into vogue in the twenty-first century. It was one of the Roman virtues that was especially appreciated in leaders. According to Wikipedia, gravitas connotes weight, seriousness, dignity ... and "a certain substance or *depth of personality"* (italics added—I love the *depth of personality* part, even though we are on the topic of the Authority/width dimension!). The *Cambridge Dictionary* defines gravitas as "seriousness and importance of manner, causing feelings of respect and trust in others." Clearly, a successful leader will need **gravitas** as an **Authority** trait at appropriate times.

> *If a rhinoceros were to enter this restaurant now, there is no denying he would have great power here. But I should be the first to rise and assure him that he had no authority whatever.*
> *(GK Chesterton to Alexander Woollcott)*

In chapter 1 you were introduced to a basic explanation of three dimensions. My hope is that, after reading that chapter, you have come to think of leadership in the dimensions of *height, width, and depth.* Notice that when anyone refers to three dimensions they almost always mention *height* first. I'm not sure why that is, but it just might have something to do with human nature. Height is perhaps what first impresses us when we look at or visualize something. For instance, right now think of a tree. Most of us will subconsciously decide how *tall* that tree will be before we assign any other characteristics to our vision.

Measuring Authority

Recall the **Dimensional Properties** that were presented in chapter 1. In terms of height,

- the first one was that **the only measure of height is the distance from one point to another;**
- then, **there is no limit to the potential measurement of height—it can be infinite;**
- third, **higher is not necessarily better (than something less high).**

The fourth Dimensional Property states that **width and height are most effectively illustrated when width is greater than height, in a ratio of approximately 16:9.**

These properties apply to the dimension of Authority just as they do to the dimension of height. You can measure the amount of Authority a person has, except it is a subjective measurement rather than objective. You can't say that a certain leader has ten units of Authority, but still there are low and high points of Authority that you can sense. Further, the potential of Authority is limitless, and more Authority is not necessarily better than less Authority.

I need to interject here a point about my approach to the concept of 3-D and Tree-Dimensional Leadership. Experts have developed all sorts of written instruments for measuring facets of leadership. They invest a great deal of time attempting to validate those instruments so that they can be considered "the gospel truth." They print them up in fancy designs with complicated scoring mechanisms and then send highly-paid consultants to administer the instruments to a company's employees. The employees study multiple-page profiles of tables and charts about themselves, find details they already know, and then forget those details by the next day. My view of what matters most in any sort of analysis is what you can understand

and remember. You won't find any detailed written instruments to measure my version of 3-D Leadership. I use common sense thought processes that anyone can apply in any setting—and they are free! (I will, however, still be happy to come to your organization for an exorbitant fee and explain **Tree-Dimensional Leadership**. *The difference is the participants will easily understand the concept, and will remember it forever!)*

So whether you are analyzing your own Authority or someone else's, you simply decide how "high" the Authority is and visualize it in your mind. You can draw a picture or chart if it will help. Remember that I want you to be thinking about leadership in 3-D now, so let's use the three-dimensional box for your mental picture. You might want to use one illustration as a standard, and another to represent the reality of yourself or someone you are rating, like this:

Your standard for Authority

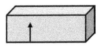

Your impression of a person with low Authority (16:9, remember?)

(In these examples we are ignoring the Ability and Character dimensions.)

Your impression of a person with high Authority

Bear with me as I gradually introduce you to the real leadership model of this book, *Tree-Dimensional Leadership*. We are starting out using a 3-D box to help you learn the content and interactions of 3-D Leadership. But this is just a stepping stone to using the image of a noble tree to represent everything about Leadership. A tree is a living thing and capable of so much imagery that you will find it a fascinating way to envision, remember, and assess Leadership.

Remember that *in general* the ratio of width to height is more "pleasant and/or effective" when width is slightly greater than height. Translated to 3-D Leadership, this means that a person should in general—most of the time and in a broad sense—exhibit less Authority than Abilities. Specific situations, though, may call for a demonstration of strong Authority. For example, a military squad leader may be more effective by immediately standing up to an insubordinate soldier than by taking the time to demonstrate that he knows the best way to cross the river.

Using Authority

You might remember my earlier example of a cave man using a club as the original exercise of Leadership. Authority, in my opinion, is the original and fundamental Dimension of Leadership. We expect leaders to have and exercise Authority; we have elaborate systems for recruiting, selecting, electing, and otherwise placing people in positions of Authority; and we generally applaud those who scratch and claw their way to such positions. The use of Authority can create a love-hate relationship between a leader and those being led. The devil, as they say, is in the details. We like an authoritative leader when he is getting the things done that we want in the way that we want. A highly authoritative leader, especially in an opposing camp, can be interpreted as a monster; and even our own leader isn't so cool if she runs roughshod over "the little people."

You do not lead by hitting people over the head—that's assault, not leadership.
(Dwight D. Eisenhower)

Authority should be seen as a part of leadership, not as a way around it.
(Michael McKinney)

Up to this point, we have been discussing Authority as if it were a single trait of Leadership. It is, however, a *category* of traits, components, elements or factors that are associated with Authority. Most often I will use the term *traits* to represent components of each dimension but such components can be a variety of things that include descriptors (adjectives), actions (verbs), or things (nouns). **If you make a list of every trait or characteristic that describes a leader, you will find that they can all be sorted into the three categories of <u>Authority</u>, <u>Abilities</u>, or <u>Character</u>.** While this may seem to be a very bold statement, with some practice you will find it to be quite accurate. No model, however, can be 100 percent pure. There are a few traits that can be assigned to two or even all three categories. When this is the case, the trait will have a slightly different meaning depending on the Dimension to which it is assigned. Sometimes it will just be a matter of opinion, and that's okay. Let's look further into the Dimension of Authority by examining what you might call components of Authority.

Being powerful is like being a lady. If you have to tell people you are, you aren't. (Margaret Thatcher)

- **Power** is a primary ingredient of Authority. One definition of power that I especially like is "the possession of control or command over others" (Dictionary.com). The use of power implies a kind of raw independence that does not depend on permission from others. Power is not my favorite attribute. It is rare that a leader can effectively use power without abuse. I worked once with an individual who was a master at using personal power to make other people curry his favor. He would alternate between being a person's best buddy and ignoring that person. Without knowing it, people would do anything they could to please him so that he would smile at them or bring them into his inner circle. He knew exactly what he was doing, and it served him well. He just didn't earn *my* friendship or support, but he didn't need it to get what he wanted.

- **Aggressiveness**, on the other hand, can be seen as a little less direct than plain power. It is still a component of Authority and is usually part of the arsenal of extremely Authoritative leaders.

Authority makes some people grow; with others, it just makes them swell up. (Reminisce Magazine)

- **Assertiveness** is even less direct than aggresiveness, and communicates an impression of self-respect and respect for others.
- **Determination** reinforces a person's Authority by sending a message that instills confidence in the followers. Have you ever seen a dog focused on the scent of its prey? It is nearly impossible to distract him, and there is no doubt that the dog will find what it is looking for.
- **Persistence** is similar to determination but involves a sense of "stick-to-it-iveness" rather than focus. You know that a leader with persistence will not be easily shaken or swayed.
- **Leverage** may not come readily to mind as a trait of Authority, but it can be a vital attribute. Some people seem to have a natural way of using contacts and resources to the advantage of themselves or their group. Politicians are

especially good at using leverage to obtain support for their causes, thereby increasing their Authority.

- **Position** is an absolute necessity. A leader's Authority derives from some type of position, be it elected, appointed, earned or seized. Adolph Hitler became the supreme leader of Nazi Germany through a series of successions to increasingly powerful positions of Authority. People with no previous experience or recognition as a leader have been elevated to positions of Authority simply by election or appointment. Whether or not they succeed from that point depends primarily on their other two dimensions of Abilities and Character. I observed numerous college students over the years who had not previously served in an official leadership role but were elected as presidents of clubs and even of student government associations. Some of them became outstanding leaders while others failed miserably.

- **Image** is another essential component of Authority. You communicate Authority through your image. Physical appearance, unfortunately, influences the opinions people have of you, at least initially. You are born with your basic physical image, but you can develop or adjust much that matters. Simple things like posture (your mom always told you to stand up straight) and grooming are fully in your control; and with effort you can lose weight, control your temper, and communicate a sense of strength. Voice quality can affect one's image as well. When the 2012 Republican presidential primaries were in full throttle, one of the television channels used a focus group to react to the Michigan primary, in which Rick Santorum and Mitt Romney fought tooth and nail. Santorum had almost lost his voice by the day of the primary. Addressing his supporters after the polls closed, his voice was deeper and raspier than usual. The TV commentator noted that Santorum appeared to have made the best of his altered voice, sounding a bit like Clint Eastwood as he spoke, inspiring his supporters to cheers and wild applause. Some members of the focus group agreed, saying that the quality of Santorum's delivery gave him an air of Authority. In the 1988 presidential campaign Gov. Michael Dukakis essentially knocked himself out of the race by posing in an army tank wearing a helmet that made him look like Klinger the not-to-be-taken-seriously character on M*A*S*H.

Respect commands itself and can neither be given nor withheld when it is due. (Eldridge Cleaver)

It's hard to lead a cavalry charge if you think you look funny on a horse. (Adlai Stevenson)

In the early stages of the 2016 presidendial race, Donald Trump capitalized on his public image to gain daily television exposure and ride the top of polls very quickly. (I will discuss Trump and the wild and wooly 2016 election in more depth in chapter 12.)

Of course there are many additional traits that make up the dimension of Authority. Leaders can exhibit all, some or none of them, and they can be used in one situation and not in another. The table below lists the Authority traits discussed above and a few others. Use your imagination to come up with more if you wish.

__Examples of Authority__

Gravitas	Assertiveness	Aggressiveness	Determination
Persistence	Leverage	Type of Position	Image
Influence	Confidence	Policies/Procedures	Strength
Stamina	Force	Intelligence	Prestige
Control	Boldness	Autonomy	Dominance
Power	Decisiveness	Supervisor's Latitude	Command

Mental Image of Authority

We can consider Authority, then, as the first and fundamental dimension of leadership. We can visualize a person's Authority as the *height* of an imaginary three-dimensional box, aware of but ignoring for the moment the other dimensions.

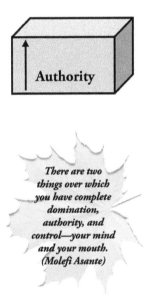

There are two things over which you have complete domination, authority, and control—your mind and your mouth. (Molefi Asante)

We can vary that height in our minds, depending on how much Authority we judge the person to have. We can also determine the sources of a person's Authority. Sometimes a leader just exudes Authority, and we are not sure why that is, but we know it is there, and we can sense how much. More often, however, we can identify certain traits that are like the fibers from which Authority is made. With practice, you can quickly size up a person's Authority dimension without any special tools or forms.

The most dangerous thing about power is to employ it where it is not applicable.
(David Halberstam)

Authority is a poor substitute for leadership.
(John L. Beckley)

Reading the Rings

Examine your dimension of Authority. Of course your exercise of Authority can vary with the situation, but think of your general Authority as a box full of traits that can be used as needed.

Using your own expectations as a standard, is your box high, medium or low? How does it compare to someone else in a similar leadership role? Now look deeper and describe the individual traits that make up your Authority.

5

Ability Represented by Width

A little bird with feathers brown
Sat singing on a tree;
The song was very soft and low,
But sweet as it could be.

And all the people passing by
Looked up to see the bird
That made the sweetest melody
That ever they had heard.

But all the bright eyes looked in vain,
For birdie was so small,
And with a modest, dark-brown coat,
He made no show at all.

"Why mamma!" little Gracie said,
"Where can the birdie be?
If I could sing a song like that,
I'd sit where folks could see."
"I hope my little girl will learn
A lesson from the bird,
And try to do what good she can,
Not to be seen or heard.

"This birdie is content to sit
Unnoticed by the way,
And sweetly sing his Maker's praise
From dawn 'til close of day.

"So live, my child, all through your life,
That, be it short or long,
Though others may forget your looks,
They'll not forget your song."

—John McCoy, MD, 1893

49

Using Abilities

I t can be said that all of us, like the little bird, have at least one special gift, skill, or talent. If we want to fulfill our potential, we need to make the best possible use of the Abilities endowed by our Creator (or developed in expensive dance or piano classes and after years of practice and recitals). Exercising such skills without appearing one-dimensional requires a special sort of balancing act. The little bird knows how. She sings her heart out, but goes about her life in an unassuming way, still attending to the necessities of self-preservation, finding food, and socializing with other birds. Effective leadership is very much like that. Abilities are essential, but they lose their impact if exercised at the expense of our other dimensions.

I believe we can fly on the wings we create.
(Melissa Etheridge)

I long to accomplish a great and noble task, but it is my chief duty to accomplish small tasks as if they were great and noble.
(Helen Keller)

At the risk of being redundant, let me remind you that 3-D Leadership is the simple *combination* of **Authority, Abilities, and Character.** Each of these dimensions is being discussed in separate chapters, but "refined" leadership can never separate the three.

We can't take any credit for our talents. It's how we use them that counts.
(Madeleine L. Engle)

A man must ... stand in some terror of his talents. A transcendent talent draws so largely on his forces as to lame him.
(Ralph Waldo Emerson)

Another point I should make is that I alternate between the use of **Ability** and **Abilities** to describe the width dimension of leadership. I use the singular to refer to the *category* of Abilities and the plural to acknowledge that the category consists of numerous individual Ability traits, components, or factors. That being said, it is important to understand that Abilities are essential to leadership.

In the previous chapter, I included a table listing examples of Authority traits. Let's look now at a list of Ability traits. Remember that some traits can "cross over" from one dimension to another. In those cases, the trait can be defined in terms of either dimension. An example might be intelligence. In the Authority dimension, intelligence refers to a fundamental, natural-born potential that others recognize, acknowledge, and defer to, strengthening the leader's Authority. On the other hand, intelligence can also be considered an Ability, in that it provides a leader with intellectual tools that can be used to accomplish goals.

Examples of Abilities

Intelligence	Timing	Planning	Organizing
Budgeting	Flexibility	Delegating	Teaching
Communication	Public Speaking	Use of Resources	Negotiating
Evaluating	Common Sense	Social Awareness	Interpreting Info.
Use of Technology	Correcting Others	Problem-solving	Anticipating
Innovation	Mathematics	Decision-making	Spatial Thinking
Learning	Reasoning	Adaptability	Resolving Conflict
Clarity	Coping	Task Effectiveness	Initiative

Of course there are many other traits that can be considered part of the Ability dimension. Those listed above are more general in nature, but very specific abilities can be just as important, such as operating a chainsaw, using a particular tool, or even skipping rope.

Often the abilities that are needed for leadership are special skills related to the type of work being done. Indeed, people are often promoted to supervisory positions because they are good at what they do. In many fields, this is important—especially if the supervisor must continue to be involved in the tasks alongside the workers, as with firemen, policemen, production line workers, and the like. Talents and skills related to the job are also generally more relevant for lower-level supervisors. The higher up the ladder one goes, the less important *job skills* become, and the more important *leadership, management,* or *supervisory skills* become.

Like the general evolution of leadership that I described earlier, the application of Abilities evolves with the scope of the leadership role. For example, when an assembly-line worker receives a promotion, he needs to be skilled *at least* in the assembly-line process. As time goes by and responsibilities increase, his Abilities need to evolve to higher levels as illustrated by this flow chart:

Assembling parts ⟶ Maintenance of machinery ⟶ Systems management ⟶ Budgeting, Personnel, and Policy management ⟶ Plant management

Far too often, people are promoted to positions of leadership *solely* because of their job skills with no consideration of their supervisory or management skills—basically the "Peter Principle" (promotion to one's level of incompetence). This invariably results in miserable employees at best and a failed organization at worst. The potential for successful Leadership must be correctly judged by both the person doing the promoting *and* the person being promoted. Both must assure themselves that the employee has at least some of all three Leadership Dimensions (Authority, Abilities and Character). Abilities are necessary, but abilities alone are simply not enough.

Shortly after I started a new job, I supervised a lady who (*bless her heart* as we say in the South) had been promoted over the years to a high-level position with responsibility for a two million dollar budget. She had started her career as a teacher, and was probably quite good at *teaching*. After several years in the high-level position and as she neared retirement, she was known as a kind and gentle lady, and her employees loved her. But her financial management skills were thin at best; her budget was running into trouble halfway through the fiscal year. Projections showed that the program was headed toward a $30,000 year-end deficit. So I called a meeting with her and her staff and suggested that we needed to take action to manage the budget to head off the impending deficit. She was quite amused at what she saw as *my* obvious inexperience with things like budgeting and patted me on the back while assuring me, "Dr. Hartzog, you should know that nobody can *manage* a budget! This happens every year, and we just ask for a special (federal) grant to cover it." (Yes, let's just borrow it from China.) To her credit, she ultimately went along with my suggestions for cutting expenses through temporary reduction of programs, operating hours, and services. *She was amazed to learn that you can make changes to a budget!* (We still, however, ended up depending on a $10,000 grant at the end of the year.) She clearly illustrated leadership with sufficient Authority and Character, but **Abilities** more suited to a lower-level supervisory position.

Many people have the ambition to succeed; they may even have special aptitude for their job. And yet they do not move ahead. Why? Perhaps they think that since they can master the job, there is no need to master themselves.
(John Stevenson)

Seek not a task to fit your ability, but the ability to fit the task.
(Reminisce Extra Magazine)

The person who knows "how" will always have a job. The person who knows "why" will always be his boss.
(Diane Ravitch)

Measuring Ability

Again, recall the **Dimensional Properties** that were presented in chapter 1. In terms of width,

- the first one was that **the only measure of width is the distance from one point to another.** Translated into leadership terms, this means that the only measure of an Ability is how much of that Ability a person may have.
- Next, **there is no limit to the potential measurement of width** (in this case, an Ability)—**it can be infinite.** I know that sounds weird, but what this means is that you can never place an actual limit on a person's Ability; as soon as you do, someone will prove you wrong by exceeding that limit. World records continue to be broken in every sport, for example.

- Third, **wider is not necessarily better (than something less wide).** Is a person a better supervisor just because she can assemble parts quickly?
- The fourth Dimensional Property states that **width and height are most effectively illustrated when width is greater than height, in a ratio of approximately 16:9.** You probably understand this in terms of 3-D images, but it may be more difficult to accept in terms of Abilities versus Authority. My model of 3-D Leadership insists, however, that an effective leader will exhibit more Abilities than Authority. Consider a leader who runs out of the Ability to do something and only has his Authority left as the quality to lead. That is what creates dictators like Idi Amin and Muammar Gaddafi.

I never learned anything while I was talking.
(Larry King)

Between falsehood and useless truth there is little difference. As gold which he cannot spend will make no man rich, so knowledge which cannot apply will make no man wise.
(Samuel Johnson)

Even a child is known by his doings, whether his work be pure, and whether it be right.
(Proverbs 20:11)

Bob Kaplan in his book *The Versatile Leader* (2006) notes that leaders can be "lopsided." They can emphasize one skill or technique to excess—or not enough. He even notes that "maximizing a value corrupts it" (p. 69). To illustrate this point, Kaplan quotes a segment of Sherwood Anderson's novel *Winesburg, Ohio*. The author is describing "grotesques," which are individuals who deform themselves by latching onto a single truth (reminiscent of my earlier reference to the novel *Flatland*):

"In the beginning when the world was young … all about in the world were the truths and they were all beautiful…. Hundreds and hundreds were the truths and they were beautiful. "And then the people came along. Each as he appeared snapped up one of the truths …

"It was the truths that made people grotesques …. The moment one of the people took one of the truths to himself, called it his truth, and tried to live by it, he became a grotesque and the truth he embraced became a falsehood."

Such are those leaders who have limited Abilities or who latch onto a single Ability to the exclusion of others. An Ability may be perfectly suited to a situation, but can be used so improperly or so excessively that it "corrupts" the situation.

Again, without the aid of expensive and time-consuming instruments, you can estimate the "width" of your own or someone else's Abilities by visualizing the width of the 3-D model:

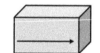
Your standard for Ability (16:9)

Impression of narrow Ability dimension.

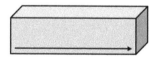

Your impression of a person with wide Ability dimension.

56

In the final analysis, the one quality that all successful people have ... is the ability to take on responsibility.
(Michael Korda)

I've gone through life believing in the strength and competence of others; never in my own. Now, dazzled, I discover that my capacities were real. It was like finding a fortune in the lining of an old coat.
(Joan Mills)

One of the great travesties of the twentieth and twenty-first centuries has been the common method of evaluating employees by grading a series of descriptors that have little to do with the actual job description of the person being evaluated. Terms such as "punctual," "flexible," "visible," and "dresses appropriately" are often used as standards on company-wide forms that are used to rate the Abilities of *all* employees, regardless of the type of work each individual is supposed to be doing. Forms used when I was in the military were especially useless. The rating official was tasked with checking one of five levels to describe such attributes as "effectiveness in working with others," "judgment," "adaptability," and—best of all—"leadership characteristics." Everyone has seemed to blindly accept this method of rating the Abilities of people—especially of rating leaders—without realizing the folly of it.

In the first place, ratings of such descriptors are purely subjective. The person administering the evaluation must use his or her own standards as to what is outstanding "flexibility," "adaptability," and so on. One rater may feel that too much "visibility" is unproductive while another may really like showy people. Such ratings will vary widely, depending on who is doing the rating. And what the heck is meant by "leadership characteristics"? I know that supervisors have rated me at levels ranging from dismal to walking on water, while the job I was doing and the manner in which I did it remained the same (which I always believed was perfect, by the way).

In the second place, ratings of personality traits simply don't have anything to do with how well the person is performing on the job. Someone who dresses appropriately may be lazy as hell and accomplishing nothing. An employee who is sometimes late to work may be the most productive person in the office. Does it *really* matter if a person is *in the office* from eight o'clock to five o'clock, if he gets more work done from eight thirty to seven? Anyone who knows me will understand why this is one of my pet peeves, as I have rarely paid close attention to a clock throughout my life. Of course I realize that certain positions require regular hours, such as a secretary who must answer phones during posted office hours, or anyone who is replacing another worker at a scheduled time. Paying more attention to a clock than your purpose or mission, however, adds nothing to the measure of your leadership.

When evaluating a person's job performance, what really matters is *the job description.* Here you have an objective, measurable set of standards that can be evaluated with relative ease, even by different people at different times. What should be measured is whether or not a person utilizes his Abilities to accomplish what he was hired to do. It is the supervisor's responsibility to craft a meaningful job description—which is done best with input from the employee, and revised as necessary. Evaluation sessions should focus on each item in the job description, not on the personal habits of the employee. For example, one of Mary's responsibilities is to maintain high office morale. Rating her high as "a cheerful person" or "punctual" would be meaningless. Noting that monthly surveys of staff morale have shown steady improvement is one pretty good indicator that she is accomplishing that part of her job description. Evaluations don't even have to use the terms "good," "excellent," or "outstanding." The measurement can simply state "accomplished" or "not accomplished" or degrees can be used such as "partially fulfilled" or "making progress toward goal." This process may not in every instance directly measure a person's abilities, but the *presence* of abilities doesn't guarantee that a job is getting done—especially if leadership is being measured. Unless it's a beauty contest, *results* are what matters.

You cannot fly like an eagle with the wings of a wren.
(William Henry Hudson)

Knowing is not enough, we must apply. Willing is not enough, we must do.
(Johann Wolfgang von Goethe)

Many of you have probably seen some version of the following parody of Abilities sought in a position announcement for a company vice president. While this one is obviously a joke, in reality it is not far off from the private thoughts of some CEO's:

Must leap tall buildings in single bounds (upon the suggestion of any other vice president).

High visibility—cape and tights preferred.

Handicapped okay—especially forked tongue and two sets of lips—so that the applicant can talk out of both sides of his mouth and kiss two asses at the same time.

Pay attention to details—because no one else here does.

Flexible—must be able to fake compassion on a regular basis.

Adaptable to sudden shifts in policy decisions.

Appreciation for aesthetics must take precedence over function.

Teamwork—willingness to subordinate own ideas and needs to any half-baked schemes of the CEO or other VP's.

Ability to assess others (adept at gossip).

Adept at fly fishing or playing bridge.

Perspective—ability to exaggerate minor problems and minimize major ones.

Familiarity with honor and integrity, but not committed to them.

Adept at human relations—good at squeezing shoulders hard, smiling, and telling everyone, "You're my good frie-ennd!"

Oh my Lord, do I have experience with that level of corporate crap! I much prefer the singing bird that you can hardly see.

Woe to those who rise early in the morning that they may run after their drinks. (Isaiah 5:11)

A foolish leader can be led astray by a corrupt inner circle. (Anonymous)

Mental Image of Ability

So we have now studied the second dimension of 3-D Leadership which is that group of traits we call **Ability**. At this point you should find it easier to visualize that dimension as the *width* of an imaginary three-dimensional box. We can now combine *height* (Authority) and *width* (Ability) to come up with this image:

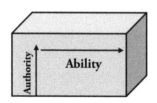

You can vary either the height or width, or both, as the mental image of your own or some other leader's Ability or Authority. A leader will have an inventory of Abilities that can be called upon singly or in various combinations. Some Abilities are stronger than others and some are used only when appropriate. Still, you can get a sense of the *overall* degree of Abilities that apply to a particular individual. A strong measure of Abilities will be represented by a *wider* box than a weaker measure would.

Hard work without talent is a shame, but talent without hard work is a tragedy.
(Robert Half)

The survivors of any species are not necessarily the strongest. And they are not necessarily the most intelligent. They are those who are most responsive to change.
(Charles Darwin)

What is important is to keep learning, to enjoy challenge, and to tolerate ambiguity. In the end there are no certain answers.
(William Henry Hudson)

Talent is something rare and beautiful and precious, and it must not be allowed to go to waste.
(George Selden)

Reading the Rings

Take stock of your arsenal of Abilities. It may help to actually make a list because there can be so many of them.

Then compare your Ability dimension with your Authority dimension by drawing them as rectangles.

Do the rectangles reflect the 16:9 aspect ratio (wider than tall)?

6

Character Represented by Depth

Character Represented by Depth

C haracter is the third dimension of leadership, represented by *depth*—the dimension that gives a leader the human touch.

The story of Pinocchio is perfectly suited to illustrate the importance of Character as the dimension of depth. The original story by Carlo Collodi, published in 1883, is rather convoluted, but Walt Disney simplified it a bit with his 1940 animated film. A live-action version with Henson (Muppet) Studio creations (depicted above) was produced by New Line Cinema in 1996. Created as a wooden puppet by his "father" Geppetto, Pinocchio is partially brought to life, but still made of wood, by a blue fairy. She tells him that he can become a real boy if he proves himself to be "brave, truthful, and unselfish" and is able to tell right from wrong by listening to his conscience. (Ah, could not all of us benefit from such attributes …) Poor Pinocchio stumbles through a series of misadventures, being led astray with bad advice from other characters and falling in with the wrong crowd. When he tells lies, his nose grows "until it is like the branch of a tree." (What a convenient metaphor for the later section of this book when we get into *Tree-Dimensional Leadership*!) Further, Pinocchio turns to gambling, smoking, getting drunk and destroying property. For such behavior he becomes a partial jackass, growing the ears and tail of a donkey. After virtually sacrificing his own life in order to save Geppetto and Geppetto's pets, Pinocchio is finally revived as a real boy by the blue fairy, and they all live happily ever after.

Leaders become "real boys" when they learn to appropriately embrace the humanizing traits of Character. Certainly a leader can function, and even succeed, by using only Authority and/or Ability. You will find, however, that the most effective and beloved leaders always demonstrate a depth of Character that sets them apart from those who rely on brute force or showy skills alone.

One of the great things about writing my own book is that I can take "poetic license" and define terms as I wish. My interpretation of Character as a Leadership Dimension is much broader than typical approaches to the word might suggest, but I am confident you will agree that my version makes perfect sense. In the context of 3-D and Tree-Dimensional Leadership, Character is the group of traits that humanize a leader. The traits include such qualities and attributes as warmth, empathy, integrity, sense of humor, emotions, self-awareness, self- control, and respect for others. Including the advice of the blue fairy, being "brave, truthful, and unselfish" and able to tell right from wrong.

African culture has long recognized the importance of Character with the concept of *Ubuntu*, which has its origin in the Bantu languages of southern Africa. The word promotes a broad and powerful philosophy that emphasizes humanity, compassion, and goodness as fundamental to the way Africans approach life. Liberian peace activist Leymah Gbowee said of Ubuntu: "I am what I am because of who you are." Archbishop Desmond Tutu explained that "one of the sayings in our country is Ubuntu—the essence of being human." Ubuntu embraces the fact that you can't exist as a human being in isolation. It implies interconnectedness. Tutu goes on to say that you can't be human all by yourself, and when you have this quality—Ubuntu—you are known for your generosity.

Judge Colin Lamont noted in a court ruling that Ubuntu is a concept which

- dictates that a high value be placed on the life of a human being;
- is inextricably linked to the values of and which places a high premium on dignity, compassion, humaneness, and respect for humanity of another;
- dictates good attitudes and shared concern;
- facilitates resolution of differences rather than conflict and victory for the most powerful; and
- favors civility and dialogue premised on mutual tolerance. *Wikipedia.org/wiki/Ubuntu_(philosophy)*

Similar concepts with different names exist throughout African culture and have been recognized by Western leaders on numerous occasions.

Botho (Ubuntu) defines a process for earning respect by first giving it, and to gain empowerment by empowering others. It encourages people to applaud rather than resent those who succeed. It disapproves of anti-social, disgraceful, inhuman and criminal behavior, and encourages social justice for all. (Botswana's Vision 2016)

The king owed his status, including all the powers associated with it, to the will of the people under him. (Stanlake J. W. T. Samkange)

"UBUNTU!"
(Chanted by the
Boston Celtics
basketball team
when breaking
huddles)

The concept of *Ubuntu*, however, is apparently not so comprehensive that it includes such traits as sense of humor and charisma, which I believe can easily be seen as some of the "humanistic" traits of Character.

In an article for *Reader's Digest* ("Why Character Counts," January 1999) author Stephen R. Covey explained that without character, you will never succeed. He described a consulting job with a bank manager who could not understand why employee morale was low and his bank was failing despite all of his efforts to motivate employees and improve the situation. After a while, Covey learned the problem was that everyone knew the manager was having an extra-marital affair with an employee. The manager had plenty of Authority and Abilities, but the problem was lack of *Character*.

It takes 20 years to build
a reputation and five
minutes to ruin it. If you
think about that, you'll
do things differently.
(Warren Buffet)

Covey goes on to say that "Character is made up of those principles and values that give your life direction, meaning *and depth*" (the italics are mine). He notes that it is out of vogue today to speak in terms of character, and that some people wonder if our inner values matter anymore. It hasn't always been that way. People like Benjamin Franklin and Thomas Jefferson made it clear that Character should be the bedrock of our lives.

In the article, Covey notes that "while skill is certainly needed for success, it can never guarantee happiness and fulfillment." You can consciously build character, and you can begin at any age. It may take great effort but will eventually become habit as you make deposits in your "character account." (In the next chapter, we will discuss in detail the difference between *natural* or inborn traits and those that can be *nurtured* for growth and improvement.)

I referred earlier to the 2012 Republican presidential primaries. One frequently-discussed shortcoming of former Governor Mitt Romney was his lack of warmth, humor, and connectedness with voters—the *human touch*, as many put it. Of course, this is a clear example of the importance of the Character Dimension of leadership. Late-night host Jimmy Fallon parodied that impression of Romney with a skit on his show in which the term "I, Robot" (referring to the Will Smith movie about robots taking over the world) was matched with the phrase "how Mitt Romney began his wedding vows." Generally, people don't look favorably on a leader who is stiff and robot-like. People prefer someone with whom they can connect, who can be "like one of them." During the 2016 presidential race, I don't think *anyone* accused Donald Trump of being predictable or like a robot!

You can be totally rational with a machine. But, if you work with people, sometimes logic has to take a back seat to understanding.
(Akio Morita)

I believe that the details of our lives will be forgotten by most, but the emotion, the spirit, will linger with those who shared it, and be part of them forever.
(Liv Ullmann)

Good-tempered leaders invigorate lives; they're like spring rain and sunshine.
(Proverbs 16:15)

Laughter is the shortest distance between two people.
(Victor Borge)

Make happy those who are near, and those who are far will come.
(Chinese Proverb)

If you think about what you ought to do for other people, your character will take care of itself.
(Woodrow Wilson)

Tim Sanders wrote an engaging book titled *The Likeability Factor* (2006), in which he addresses the importance of being liked by other people. Likeability, he says, "is more than important, it's more than practical, it's more than appealing. Likeability may well be the deciding factor in every competition you'll ever enter." I highly recommend this book to anyone who thinks they may need a little help in this area.

The L-Factor, as he calls it, is comprised of four basic elements:

- Friendliness
- Relevance
- Empathy
- Realness

Sanders provides some excellent advice on how to raise your L-Factor in each of these areas. Each element poses challenges that can require focus and effort, but the effort must become natural—otherwise your actions can come across as contrived, and the result is *unlikeability*. In most cases the elements of likeability are best communicated person-to-person in face-to-face encounters. How, for example, can a politician exhibit likeability without "pressing the flesh" by shaking hands, kissing babies, and such? The age of television and YouTube has actually made genuine likeability more difficult to convey or judge because what voters see on their screens are not necessarily the *real* images of the people being observed.

The only way to have a friend is to be one.
(Ralph Waldo Emerson)

An important difference between Character and the other two dimensions is that Character *guides* the use or expression of Abilities and Authority. Character traits are often not visible themselves, but can be inferred from the actual actions of Authority or Abilities. For example, when a leader uses his Authority to correct an injustice, the action is more than likely (invisibly) motivated by the Character trait of compassion. On the other hand, there are devious leaders who would take such action merely to exercise or demonstrate their Authority—which still can be attributed to a Character trait, albeit a *negative* one such as selfish pride.

This *guiding* nature of Character can be compared to the function of a ship's rudder, which is not seen from the surface, while the sails represent Ability and the hull Authority. Hey, there's a neat model: LeaderSHIP (but I will stick with *Tree*-Dimensional Leadership).

Using Character

I'm not crazy about the concept of *using* Character, because I think such traits should be the fundamental guides for everything a leader does—actions that come from the heart and that are instinctive, not polished up and displayed *over* the heart like jewelry. When a person seems to be *using* Character traits, he loses credibility quickly. Sometimes faked Character is immediately obvious, but in other cases, it takes years to be discovered. Politicians and high-profile executives are two of the most obvious groups that provide clear examples. Just think of leaders like Richard Nixon, John Kennedy, Bill Clinton, Richard Madoff, and John Edwards—all of whom portrayed public images of the highest Character, but eventually had very compromising parts of their lives revealed. Fans of Presidents Kennedy and Clinton may furrow their brows, as a recent poll showed both were rated highly for charisma as presidents, in spite of affairs (three now reported for Kennedy and at least one for Clinton).

The challenge of leadership is to be strong but not rude; be kind but not weak; be bold, but not a bully; be thoughtful, but not lazy; be humble, but not timid; be proud, but not arrogant; have humor, but without folly. (Jim Rohn, motivational speaker)

The shortest and surest way to live with honor in the world is to be in reality what we would appear to be; all human virtues increase and strengthen themselves by the practice and experience of them. (Ralph Waldo Emerson)

Let's take a look at some specific Character traits, and how they are used to enhance leadership:

- **Charisma** is that vague, almost indefinable, quality that seems to be available to only a limited number of people. *Dictionary.com* defines it as "a divinely conferred gift or power" and also says it "gives an individual influence or authority over large groups of people," and it "confers ... an unusual ability for leadership (and) worthiness of veneration." That's pretty powerful stuff.

Much has been written about this strange yet well-known quality of leadership. It's kind of like magnetism; most people are drawn to charismatic leaders as with an invisible force— but others actually find the charisma repugnant, as a magnet both attracts and repels, depending on polarity. Examples of leaders with loads of charisma include biblical characters such as Abraham, Moses, Joseph, David, and Jesus; military leaders like Generals George Patton, Douglas McArthur, and Adolf Hitler; and political folk like Presidents Teddy and Franklin Roosevelt, John F. Kennedy, and Barack Obama. Remember the point about magnets both attracting and repelling— there are people who have been repelled by the charisma of each of these leaders and have strongly opposed each of them.

- **Wisdom** is another Character trait that almost defies description. You can often sense when a person has wisdom, but it is impossible to measure it or to purposely attain it. A brief article in *USA Today* (4/9/09, p. 4 D) addressed such questions as "Where does wisdom come from? Is wisdom universal or culturally based? Is it uniquely human? Is it linked to age, dependent on experience, or can wisdom be taught?" Researchers concluded that there are specific regions of the brain where wisdom originates.

One of my recent Sunday school lessons centered around wisdom as playing a key role alongside God in the Creation. Selected verses from Proverbs 8 provide a beautiful visual image of this (written from the point of view of *wisdom*):

> *The Lord created me at the beginning of His work, the first of His acts of long ago.*
> *…when He had not yet made earth and fields, or the world's first bits of soil.*
> *When He established the heavens, I was there, when He drew a circle on the face of the deep,*
> *…then I was beside Him, like a master worker;*
> *…delighting in the human race.*
> *And now, my children, listen to me; happy are those who keep my ways.*
> *Hear instruction and be wise, and do not neglect it.*

Wisdom is not the same as knowledge. Wisdom *applies* knowledge, uses prudent and careful thought, finds the right path and makes the right (or best, at least) choice. I have always felt that wisdom comes with age and experience. Children in general don't have wisdom (although there can be rare exceptions), and some people never gain a whit of it, regardless of their age.

*May I govern my passion
with absolute sway, And
grow wiser and better as
my strength wears away.*
(Walter Pope)

- **Discernment**, meaning acuteness of judgment and under-standing, is a component of wisdom. Discernment is essential to knowing the *why* rather than the *how*. Discerning people can see through false values and the smokescreens people throw up; they have the faculty of discovering the truth. In the Bible, the sons of Issachar are described in 1 Chronicles as men who "had understanding of the times, to know what Israel ought to do." The sons of Issachar understood three factors:
  ○ The culture: the population and the place where they lived.
  ○ The timing: when to move.
  ○ The strategy: the steps to take.

- **A sense of humor** has been described as the main differ-ence between humans and other creatures. Fortunately most people have this Character trait, but I have known some who don't, and many whose sense of humor was poorly-developed, odd, or twisted. Some people laugh uproariously at the slightest of jokes; some just never get it; and some get their greatest kicks at the expense of other people. I once worked with a high-level college executive who had the annoying habit of snorting when he laughed. And he rarely laughed unless another person was the focus of the joke. There was a young black man on the grounds crew (let's call him Jacob) who had a slight speech impedi-ment and was perhaps a little mentally impaired. But Jacob was loved by the students and faculty members because he always had a smile on his face and he was interested in what they were doing. So he often took longer to get from one place to another because he stopped to talk. In a meeting of the president's staff, where we discussed budgets, policy decisions and the like, the "snorter" vice president brought up the fact that he had set up an elaborate plan to have Jacob monitored by people using stopwatches and communicating with walkie-talkies (*snort, snort*). They were to send Jacob on a mission from one side of the campus to the other, and secretly time him. Reports were to be made to the snorter so that he could use the evidence to justify firing Jacob. A couple of days later, Mr. Snort, quite disappointed, told us that Jacob had gotten another job before he could fire him. Then after about two weeks, he gleefully reported that Jacob, after a few days on his new job, had *broken his arm and lost that job! (Snort, snort, snort.)* It would be a stretch to find a sense of humor in that executive's Character dimension, but as you may guess, there are positive and negative Character traits—more on that later.

- **An important part of humor** is not taking yourself too seriously—laughing at yourself once in a while. Laughter makes you and everyone around you feel good, and it breeds resilience. The key to a good sense of humor, as with most leadership traits, may largely be a matter of timing. Use of humor is not always appropriate, but at the right time a good laugh can defuse the tensest of situations. Bad timing can ruin a perfect moment. Of course moderation is almost always appropriate. A sense of humor conveys happiness, self- confidence, and approachability.

There was once a cantankerous old man who lived on a farm with his wife and two sons. The old man was just plain mean. He beat his wife and nagged at her constantly, and he did the same to his two sons. As soon as the sons got old enough they moved out and lived on their own.

One day the wife called the sons to tell them that their father had passed away, and she needed their help to make a casket out of scrap lumber and carry it out to the pasture where he had wanted to be buried. Reluctantly, the boys agreed. As they were maneuvering the rough heavy box through the gate, it bumped the fence post hard, they dropped it, and the old man abruptly sat up, waking from his deep sleep.

Much to the family's consternation, the man lived another three or four years and continued to harass everyone he could. When he finally died for real, the boys came back and built another casket. As they approached the gate, their mother cautioned "Watch out for that fence post!"

(I couldn't help but share one of my all-time favorite jokes here. Just to demonstrate my own type of humor.)

Integrity is a word worthy of its own separate book, and in fact, there are several such books. ***It is my favorite word*** because it is so important and rich and full of meaning. Many people simply equate integrity with honesty, but it is so much more than that. Integrity means that the leader's life and words match. Integrity frames your convictions. Integrity denotes purity. Integrity is wholeness, unity and strength. Probably the person best known for true integrity is the biblical Job, who says in chapter 31, verse 6, *"Let me be weighed on honest scales, that God may know my integrity."* Job maintained his integrity through the most horrific trials imaginable, holding on to his unshakeable faith. John Maxwell, referring to integrity, says in *The Maxwell Leadership Bible* that

- o Leaders must be visionary, yet they cannot see everything in the future.
- o Instead of pretending to be in control, leaders must model being under control.
- o Leaders must model humanity and identify with the limitations of followers.
- o Leaders must model an anchored life, acting from character, not emotions.

Years ago, my wife and I had our first house built. We set it on a lot and a half, so there was a steel post in the middle of our front yard that marked one of the property lines. I could never get that post out of the ground, so it just remained there, with about three inches exposed. I often forgot about it when cutting the grass, but I was always solidly reminded of its presence when the mower blades found it. After replacing the blades several times I learned to respect that steel post, because it had *quiet, simple integrity.* The post was not aggressive; it did not attack me or extend its reach. It was just always there maintaining its ground with steely strength. That is Integrity.

> *Character is made by what you stand for; reputation, by what you fall for.*
> *(Robert Quillen)*

As with Authority and Abilities, there are many traits that can be assigned to the dimension of Character. Those discussed above and a few additional ones are listed in the following table:

<u>Examples of Character</u>

Charisma	Wisdom	Discernment	Humor
Integrity	Vision	Control	Emotions
Values	Beliefs	Morality	Honor
Responsibility	Compassion	Self-awareness	Empathy
Ethics	Gratitude	Sincerity	Enthusiasm
Initiative	Stability	Justice	Authenticity

Measuring Character

Dimensional Properties apply to Character just as they do with Authority and Ability. In terms of depth,

- **The only measure of depth is the distance from one point to another** (front to back in our box model). Following this line of reasoning, Character can be measured only by how much of it a person has.
- **The measurement of depth can be infinite.** There is no limit to the amount of Character a leader can have.
- **One measure of depth is not necessarily better or worse than another.** This property can be difficult to understand. It can be applied to either the *group of traits* that make up Character or *a single trait* like charisma. Let's say that John seems to have a huge Character dimension, but Hugo's dimension of Character is not as noticeable. John and Hugo can still be equally effective as leaders because of how each applies the totality of their three dimensions. Hugo may not need as much Character in his leadership role if it is a different role than John's. If both have the same or similar roles, then each person will have different combinations of the other two dimensions (Authority and Ability). A strong measure of a single trait is likewise not necessarily better than a lesser measure. More charisma, for example, is not always better than less charisma. And different individual Character traits can offset each other or enhance each other to reflect the totality of Character. It is important to note here that while more or less of *individual* dimensions are not necessarily better or worse, the relative measure of the three dimensions *is* important, as explained in the next Property.
- **The fourth Dimensional Property—promoting the 16:9 ratio—does not directly apply to depth.** I would simply add a corollary that *depth should be roughly equal to width.* It is difficult to visualize a physical measure of

depth because you can't really see a beginning and ending point as you can with height and width. You can achieve a greater sense of a 3-D effect, however, if the appearance of depth is really impressive as opposed to being just barely 3-D. In my 3-D Leadership model, this translates to the relationship between Character, Authority, and Abilities. The most effective leader will exhibit strong components of Character and Abilities that are not overwhelmed by Authority. This concept will become quite clear when we get into **Tree-Dimensional Leadership** in chapter 11. Really. You can trust me. Go ahead and sneak a peek at chapter 11 if you wish. Exert a little Authority and make your own rules about how to read a book.

I have made the point several times that with my book you don't get expensive or elaborate measuring devices. What you do get are simple visual models to help you gauge and remember measures of your own or someone else's leadership dimensions. So let's look at the box model used previously and add Character as depth. First, visualize a box that represents the relative measures of Authority, Ability, and Character that you feel are ideal (in you or in some other leader):

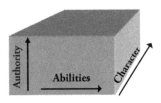

In this "ideal" figure we are representing a 16:9 ratio for Authority and Ability, and a similar ratio for Authority and Character. This would be clearer if you were somewhere in space viewing the box directly from the side. If you leave Authority and Ability ratios the same, you can visualize less desirable measures for Character as follows:

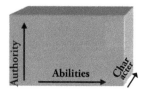

Impression of a person with low Character

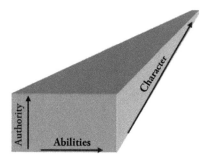

Impression of a person with extreme Character

Rudyard Kipling's magnificent poem *"IF,"* first published in 1909, is the most comprehensive guide to Character that I can imagine. Here are some selected lines:

> *If you can keep your head when all about you*
> *Are losing theirs and blaming it on you;*
> *If you can trust yourself when all men doubt you,*
> *But make allowance for their doubting too:*
> *If you can dream—and not make dreams your master;*
> *If you can think—and not make thoughts your aim,*
> *If you can talk with crowds and keep your virtue,*
> *Or walk with Kings—nor lose the common touch,*
> *If neither foes nor loving friends can hurt you,*
> *If all men count with you, but none too much;*
> *If you can fill the unforgiving minute*
> *With sixty seconds' worth of distance run,*
> *Yours is the Earth and everything that's in it,*
> *And—which is more—you'll be a Man, my son!*

John Maxwell, in his devotional guide *A Leader's Heart*, speaks about work of real value. He says that leaders must ask themselves whether they want survival, success or significance. You might even say that these three S-words parallel the three dimensions: Authority can ensure *Survival* and Ability can bring *Success,* but only Character can provide *Significance.*

Mental Image of Character

It is appropriate that the third Dimension of Leadership is more complex than the first two, as it is in the physical world. Depth is simply richer, more complicated, more meaningful even, than height or width. Character is less visible, yet more powerful and more vital than Authority or Abilities. Using the 3-D box model, it is more difficult to convey a simple image for the concept of depth, which is exactly why I came up with the progression to *Tree-* Dimensional Leadership. In the final analysis, my purpose is to provide you with a simple, easy-to-remember, yet comprehensive concept of leadership. So after this final example using a 3-D box, we will move to the tree model in chapter 11.

Now that we have *three* dimensions to see in our mind's eye, it may take a little more effort and even be a little fuzzy, but you can still visually portray Authority, Ability, and Character as this:

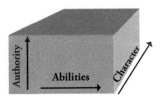

Any or all of the three dimensions can be adjusted, which changes the desirability of the shape—and this is exactly what happens when leaders exhibit different combinations of Authority, Abilities, and Character. The most effective, desirable, and significant ratio is roughly comparable to sixteen for Ability and Character, and nine for Authority—the best leadership is wider and deeper than tall. Simple as that.

In terms of human leadership, skill is the ten percent of leadership that is visible for all to see; the remaining ninety percent is comprised of character. It will be the character of the leader that sinks the ship.
(Tim Elmore)

It's not charisma, or barnstorming antics, or grand pronouncements that make a great leader; it's a very real concern and respect for people at every level of the organization—and the courage to act in their interest.
(Beverly Kaye)

Character is perfectly educated will.
(Novalis)

Character is a diamond that scratches every other stone.
(Cyrus A. Bartol)

When you meet a man, you judge him by his clothes; when you leave, you judge him by his heart.
(Russian Proverb)

Reading the Rings

Think of your favorite, most outstanding leader from the past. What was his or her Character dimension like?

Now think of a recent, emerging leader that you admire. Compare the Character of this leader with the Character of the leader from the past.

7

Nature/Nurture Factor

While debates may rage among scholars, it just seems plain common sense to me that some leadership traits can be natural-born and some can be developed, learned, or improved upon. Relying only on nature's gifts, however, will rarely be enough to succeed as a leader.

Israel Dupont submerged in the marsh with baby alligators. Photo by Ronald Dupont Jr.

Most of our problems can be solved. Some of them will take brains, and some of them will take patience, but all of them will have to be wrestled with like an alligator in the swamp.
(Harold Washington)

On the other hand ...

When you're up to your ass in alligators, it's difficult to remember that your initial objective was to drain the swamp.
(Some Smart Person)

Here's the thing: All of us are born with at least *some* natural talents, attributes, and personality traits. We know that inborn skills exist. Sometimes they can be miraculous. How do you explain it when a young child sits at a piano for the first time and plays a beautiful concerto, or when your brother is a math whiz while you are a gifted artist?

But if we relied exclusively on our inborn traits, none of us would amount to much. We have the capacity—indeed the responsibility—to improve the traits we have, and to develop others that are needed to round out our lives. Growth is something that happens to all of us, yet few actually try to manage that process. Leo Tolstoy said, "Everyone thinks of changing the world, but no one thinks of changing himself."

The individual traits within each of the three dimensions of leadership can be placed somewhere along a continuum from Nature to Nurture, where Nature is one end of a spectrum with factors that are inborn or granted and Nurture is the other end with factors that are learned, earned, or otherwise gained by effort. Here is a graphic depiction:

<u>Nature</u>

*(Traits or characteristics that are inborn or hereditary,
or factors that are set in writing or granted)*

<u>Nurture</u>

*(Traits or characteristics that are learned or developed, or
components that are earned or improved by practice)*

*In odd days like these ...
people study how to be
all alike instead of how
to be as different as they
really are.
(Monica Shannon Dobry)*

Nature/Nurture and Authority

It is vital to understand that while some traits or elements of leadership may be inborn or granted, you *have control over others.* Let's focus first on the dimension of Authority. When a person assumes a position of leadership, a continuum of elements related to that person's Authority comes into play. Those elements range from relatively fixed "gifts" to very flexible factors that can be changed or controlled by the leader.

Initially most leadership roles are rather firmly defined by the **type of position** (president, treasurer, coach, teacher, principal, etc.). Those positions are officially described in such documents as **job descriptions, bylaws,** and **organizational policies**. Beyond that, supervisors or other types of superiors determine the amount and type of Authority the leader will have, and this is a little less fixed than the foundation of written rules. Then there is the support or lack of it that comes from **peers**—other leaders on the same level. At this level there are some fixed concepts and some that are informal and more flexible. Finally, some parts of Authority can be determined from the bottom up—by the amount of support, faith, and confidence that comes from **subordinates** or other followers. Authority at this level is often determined largely by the actions of the leader and the reactions of those being led—factors that can be *Nurtured*. An adept leader will recognize where *all* sources of Authority come from, and how much flexibility there is within each category. A graphic depiction of the foregoing concepts may help:

Elements of Authority

- Type (nature) of position
- Job description
- By-laws and policies
- Support of supervisor(s)
- Support of peers
- Support of subordinates

Nature

Nurture

The same kind of Nature/Nurture continuum can be depicted for individual Authority traits such as those listed in the table on page 48 (**Examples of Authority**). For the sake of simplicity, I have listed only some of those traits in the example below, which demonstrates that **power** is probably much more fixed than **stamina**, and that **image** is more flexible or changeable than any of those listed:

Examples of Authority Traits

- Power
- Strength
- Dominance
- Stamina
- Aggressiveness
- Persistence
- Control
- Image

Nature

Nurture

The important thing is this: to be able at any moment to sacrifice what you are for what you could become.
(Charles du Bois)

When a leader recognizes the "secret" that at least some traits, factors and components of Authority can be adjusted, the leader has already enhanced his or her **Control** factor. It is simply a matter of choices. You can choose to accept the amount of Authority that is dealt to you, or you can choose to make some changes. If your job does not provide you with enough Authority to get things done, you have several options:

- Seek changes in your job description, or lobby for changes to by-laws, policies, or procedures that impact your Authority.
- Ask your supervisor for more Authority.
- Work to enlist the support of your peers for more Authority.
- Change how you supervise your subordinates so that they more readily recognize your Authority.
- If all else fails, *change jobs!*

Sometimes the impetus for change can come from outside yourself. Listening to other people can be an important tool for self-improvement. In the Book of Proverbs (19:20), the Bible says, "Pay attention to advice and accept correction." On the other hand, Ecclesiastes 7:21 says, "Do not give heed to *everything* people say, or you may hear your servant cursing you!" God certainly demonstrated time and again that when His people strayed from His ways, correction was necessary. Proverbs 13:24 reads, "If you love your children, you will correct them."

It's not our disadvantages or shortcomings that are ridiculous, but rather the studious way we try to hide them, and our desire to act as if they did not exist. (Giacomo Leopardi, 1798–1837)

A specific action is not always necessary to effect a change in your Authority dimension. Sometimes a new *attitude* will bring about the results you might need. You might, for example, simply adjust how you view or value your subordinates. Studies have shown that employees often respond positively to *intrinsic* rewards such as empowerment. Delegation of Authority to followers can improve how they relate to you, and can actually improve the image they have of you. So by adjusting your attitude and releasing some of your own Authority, you can realize a return on that investment.

It is not always by plugging away at a difficulty and sticking to it that one overcomes it; often it is by working on the one next to it. Some things and some people have to be approached obliquely, at an angle. (Andre Gide)

Nature/Nurture and Ability

Ability traits and characteristics can be arranged in a Nature/Nurture continuum just as the components of authority can. Look back at the **Examples of Abilities** listed on page 52. In that table, the traits are randomly arranged, so let's extract a few of them and create a Nature/Nurture continuum:

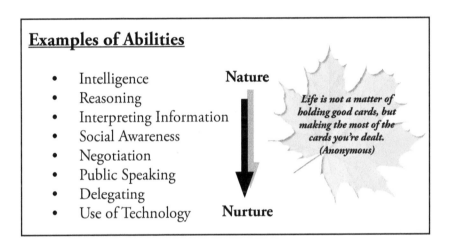

Examples of Abilities

- Intelligence
- Reasoning
- Interpreting Information
- Social Awareness
- Negotiation
- Public Speaking
- Delegating
- Use of Technology

Nature

Nurture

Life is not a matter of holding good cards, but making the most of the cards you're dealt.
(Anonymous)

The nature of **intelligence** has long been debated, and there is plenty of evidence that we are born with some and can actually develop some. We probably can all agree that each person is born with a natural *foundation* of intelligence. By the time a person becomes an adult, it is hard to tell how much intelligence was acquired over the years and how much simply grew along with the brain. My position is that most of our intelligence derives from that original foundation. Effort and environmental changes can improve it, but there is not nearly as much flexibility with traits such as intelligence and **reasoning** as there is with more skill-related traits as the ability to **speak in public** or to **use technology**.

As with Authority, the important thing for leaders to recognize is that we all start out with certain Ability traits, characteristics, and leadership factors, but we must take inventory from time to time to determine if we can improve some or need to go out and acquire others. The edge belongs to those leaders who make the most of the cards they are dealt—and who trade some in or ask for more.

Leaders can improve their Abilities in all sorts of ways. A person from one department who is promoted to a supervisory position over additional departments can (indeed, must) learn as much as possible about those other areas. When a politician is elected to a position of public service, he or she is obligated to meet with constituents, observe firsthand the problems and needs of the people, and learn as much as possible about ways to address concerns. One of the worst (and sadly, common) mistakes government officials make is to assume that their election is some sort of reward that entitles them to admiration and respect. *Hell no! Getting elected is just the beginning of your work and responsibility, you arrogant, selfish scumbag!* I'm sorry ... Where was I?

Oh yes. Just remember:

- Figure out what your natural Abilities are.
- Use them well.
- Make improvements where you can.
- Develop new skills to meet particular needs or to enhance your overall Ability Dimension.

Distinction is the consequence, never the object, of a great mind.
(Washington Allston, poet and painter)

Bloom where you're planted.
(Author Unknown)

Nature/Nurture and Character

By now I hope you are beginning to easily understand how Nature/Nurture affects the dimensions of leadership. The third dimension of Character works the same way as the other two dimensions. Look back at the examples of Character on page 75. Now let's extract a few of those examples to illustrate the Nature/Nurture concept:

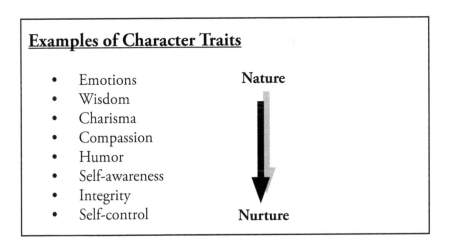

Examples of Character Traits

- Emotions
- Wisdom
- Charisma
- Compassion
- Humor
- Self-awareness
- Integrity
- Self-control

Nature

Nurture

These continuums are admittedly just my own creation and are not based on any scientific analysis. It makes perfect sense to me, however, that our **emotions** seem for the most part to come from somewhere deep within our subconscious, and they are difficult to control. Some people become very good at suppressing emotions, but the emotions are still there. Further, it is nearly impossible to *create* or even to *enhance* emotions. Lots of people try to *fake* them though.

I will probably make some political enemies here, but I can't help but refer back to the Republican presidential primaries of 2012, when Mitt Romney was often characterized as lacking emotion. In my opinion the Fox television network tried very hard to paint some emotions on Romney's image whenever they could. Mike Huckabee produced a program in which a panelist, David McArthur, tugged at viewer's hearts with an emotional explanation of his son's problems as a veteran. For weeks after that show it seemed to me that Fox ranted on and on about Gov. Romney's "emotional response" to the man's story. In my view Romney's response was a very standard and almost scripted "my heart goes out to you" kind of statement. His facial expression was as wooden as ever. Fox replayed that program more times than I thought necessary, and in a promotion of it used a clip of Romney making a slight grimace immediately after Mr. McArthur's question to the candidates. The problem is that the grimace was apparently taken from *some other portion of the program* just to paint an "emotional response" on Romney's face! (The grimace was so slight you could hardly see it; that was probably the best the network could come up with, or perhaps they didn't want the splice to be very obvious.) Now that is trying to *create* emotion, and it just doesn't work.

> *The true test of character is not how much we know how to do, but how we behave when we don't know what to do.*
> (John Holt)

During the presidential campaign in 2015, Gov. Jeb Bush and Dr. Ben Carson were painted (especially by Donald Trump) as lacking the energy to even summon up emotions. Subsequently they clearly attempted to energize their images, but their efforts were rather obviously contrived. Trump, on the other hand, openly demonstrated that he was an *entertainer*, and unabashedly exaggerated nearly everything he said, and for the most part, got away with it. Usually, Mr. Trump was *exaggerating*, rather than *faking*, and with the full understanding of his supporters, at least (it was "Huuge!").

As we move through the continuum, we can sense that traits like **wisdom** may be in our nature (or not), but can change with time and experience. I said earlier that wisdom is rarely apparent in young people. It may be that wisdom is still in their nature, but it blossoms only after a certain stage of years and experience like a century plant.

Some people have natural **charisma** but find ways to especially enhance it with things like wardrobe, hair style (anyone mentioned above come to mind?), choosing topics that strike a special chord with the audience, and selecting the best time and place to use their charisma. **Self-awareness** implies knowledge of one's traits, feelings, and behaviors. Further, it implies that you are aware of how your own attributes are connected to the world around you. I placed self-awareness toward the Nurture end of the spectrum because with just a little effort you can assess your own characteristics and make the necessary connections.

Finally (from the examples above), the trait of **self-control** is listed as the most "nurturable." The term itself indicates that you are the one who controls—it is up to *you* to reign in your temper, to curb negative urges, and to live, laugh and love as you should.

Keep in mind that there are far more leadership traits than those listed in the examples discussed above. You can decide where your own traits fit in the Nature/Nurture continuum.

Applying Nature/Nurture to Leadership

When you are not practicing, remember, someone somewhere is practicing, and when you meet him he will win.
(Ed Macauley)

Hopefully this focus on the difference between fundamental traits and those that can be more easily developed or enhanced will make you more aware of developing your potential. We must acknowledge and be grateful for whatever gifts we have, but we must also acknowledge our weaknesses and be willing to make improvements.

John Maxwell, in *A Leader's Heart,* says some people think that the best way to improve children's ability is to puff up their self-esteem because high achievers tend to have high self- esteem. Researchers have found, however, that simply building egos breeds many negative traits such as indifference to excellence, inability to overcome adversity, and aggressiveness toward people who criticize them. Surely this finding applies equally to adults, and especially to those in positions of high-level leadership. The court case of former presidential candidate John Edwards provides a classic example. What a sad state of affairs! (Pardon the pun.) John Edwards probably had his self-esteem stroked so often by so many people that he, like many other politicians, began to believe that he was invincible.

Certainly *some* promotion of self-esteem can be helpful. Children need it to help learn their worth. Adults need it to reinforce the good things in their lives. Even politicians and business leaders need it to help sustain their efforts for the public good. Just don't boost the self-esteem of a selfish, arrogant … well, I won't go there again.

Even if we become fully aware that some traits are fixed and some can be developed, it is not always easy to step outside our comfort zones and reach higher. Sometimes it takes great effort, sometimes it comes by a flash of inspiration, and often it takes courage. But that is why there is only a limited supply of great leaders.

Character cannot be developed in ease and quiet. Only through experience of trial and suffering can the soul be strengthened, ambition inspired, and success achieved.
(Helen Keller)

The leadership instinct you are born with is the backbone. You develop the funny bone and the wishbone that go with it.
(Elaine Agather)

Wisdom lies neither in fixity nor in change, but in the dialectic between the two.
(Octavio Paz)

If you create an act, you create a habit. If you create a habit, you create a character. If you create a character, you create a destiny.
(Andre Maurois)

You are not judged by the height you have risen, but from the depth you have climbed.
(Frederick Douglass, abolitionist)

Don't be afraid to take a big step if one is indicated. You can't cross a chasm in two small jumps.
(David Lloyd George, former prime minister of Great Britain)

Nothing in life is more exciting and rewarding than the sudden flash of insight that leaves you a changed person, not only changed, but for the better.
(Arthur Gordon)

Reading the Rings

Imagine yourself as a beautiful three-dimensional garden, with rich soil, large smooth stones, and lovely plants. Realize that the soil can be tilled, the stones can be aesthetically arranged, and the plants can be watered, nourished, pruned and harvested.

Always make the best of Nature and Nurture!

8

Positive/Negative Factor

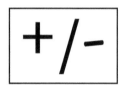

➤ Since my last report, this employee has reached rock bottom and has started to dig.

➤ Works well when under constant supervision and cornered like a rat caught in a trap.

➤ When she opens her mouth, it seems that it is only to change feet.

➤ This young lady has delusions of adequacy.

➤ He sets low personal standards and then consistently fails to achieve them.

➤ This employee is depriving a village somewhere of an idiot.

➤ This employee should go far, and the sooner he starts the better.

➤ Got a full six-pack, but lacks the plastic thing to hold it all together.

➤ He doesn't have ulcers, but he's a carrier.

➤ I would like to go hunting with him sometime.

➤ He brings a lot of joy whenever he leaves the room.

➤ When his IQ reaches fifty, he should sell.

➤ If you see two people talking and one looks bored, he's the other one.

➤ Gates are down, the lights are flashing, but the train isn't coming.

➤ If you stand close enough to him, you can hear the ocean.

➤ Some drank from the fountain of knowledge—he only gargled.

➤ Takes him two hours to watch 60 Minutes.

When I found these quotes on the internet several years ago, I was skeptical that, as the source claimed, they were from actual Federal Employee Performance Evaluations. After revelations of the past few years relating to federal agency mismanagement, overspending and corruption, however, I am certain the source was correct.

Positive and Negative factors as discussed in this chapter do not refer to the *amount* or *measure* of leadership dimensions or traits. I am talking more about *how* traits are used, and the effect such use has on leadership outcomes. (One of the **Dimensional Properties** introduced in chapter 1 states that more of a dimension is neither better nor worse than less of that dimension. For example, taller is not better than shorter just because it is taller, nor is less Authority necessarily worse than more Authority. What matters in the framework of this property is that the *situation* determines the most effective degree of the dimension. The current chapter's focus on Positive/Negative factors is not about quantitative measures of leadership traits.)

In a sense, the notes about employees quoted above can be interpreted as attempts at positive uses of negative information. While these examples are not practical for actual use, they do demonstrate that there *are* times when people say one thing and mean another. Sometimes it is done to spare feelings, and other times it is intended to mask an underlying negative tone. Quite often letters of recommendation are simply less obvious versions of these quotes.

The dynamic between positives and negatives is almost universal among ideas, concepts, and theories. Our physical world is built on it: Magnetism has positive and negative poles that attract and repel; atomic theory refers to electrons, protons and neutrons with negative, positive, and neutral qualities. We say that "opposites attract" or that things are "clear as black and white" or they are "greener on the other side"; we make comparisons of strong or weak, fast or slow, smart or dumb, funny or not—probably far more often than we should.

Most of us are familiar with the Asian/Chinese philosophy of *Yin-Yang*, which is often thought to represent the interrelationship of opposites, but it actually implies interplay of *complementary* elements of life such as ebb and flow, high tide/low tide, the swing of a pendulum, etc., represented by this symbol:

However we may view Positive/Negative factors, it is important to be aware that each of the three Dimensions of Leadership (**Authority, Ability,** and **Character**) can be applied and/or viewed in Positive or Negative terms. Further, the same concept applies to essentially every individual trait, characteristic or factor within each dimension. An effective leader will recognize the potential of Positive and Negative factors, and will realize that there is a *continuum*, or series of steps, between the two. Few concepts are absolute, so it would be rare for leadership dimensions or traits to be completely Positive or completely Negative. Normally they can be described as somewhere between the two extremes.

The test of a first-rate intelligence is the ability to hold two opposed ideas in mind at the same time and still retain the ability to function.
(F. Scott Fitzgerald)

In this chapter, we will address only the big picture, referring to the three dimensions of **Authority**, **Ability**, and **Character**. Any or all of the three can be described as Positive or Negative, either in general or in reference to a specific act. The concept can of course be applied to the individual traits, characteristics and components *within* each dimension, but addressing all of those is not really necessary to get the point across.

Positive/Negative Authority

Certain leaders throughout history seem to be surrounded with either Positive or Negative auras. For Christians, Jesus represents the ultimate Positive force in the world. He is one of the rare exceptions where *absolute* Positive applies. To Christians, at least, there is no Negative in Jesus, even when in anger he overturned tables, set free sacrificial animals, and completely disrupted the sacred temple. Jesus represents love, light, and all that is good in the world. He has attracted hosts of followers, not only in his own time, but throughout history.

> *And the Word became flesh and dwelt among us, and we beheld His glory, the glory as of the only begotten of the Father, full of grace and truth.*
> *(John 1:14, NKJV)*

Unfortunately there is an abundance of leaders who have demonstrated Negative auras. Many well-known examples will come to mind, such as Adolf Hitler, Saddam Hussein, Attila the Hun, Muammar Gaddafi, and one of my "favorites" Idi Amin Dada Oumee (AKA "Big Daddy," AKA "Butcher of Africa," AKA "Conqueror of the British Empire," and AKA "Lord of all Beasts of the Earth and

Fishes of the Sea.") Using a personal example, however, let me tell you a tale of two Air Force base commanders.

In the 1970s I was assigned to a position on a base that offered much that my wife, toddler son and I were excited about. My job as special services officer (rank of captain) involved supervising all the fun things on the base: the movie theater, golf course, swimming pool, bowling lanes, and other recreation programs. The base commander was a kindly, grandfather-like gentleman who was loved and respected by all. Colonel Rogers even reminded me of *Mr.* Rogers of "Welcome to my Neighborhood" fame. For a few months, the positive attitude and gentle leadership of Colonel Rogers resulted in a smoothly-run, efficient, and effective base operation. His retirement ceremony reflected the love and respect felt by all who reported to him.

Then came the military version of the Antichrist. I will refer to him as Colonel Queeg in allusion to the nefarious Navy captain in *The Caine Mutiny.* Colonel Queeg arrived in the middle of the night when I had the unfortunate monthly assignment as "officer of the day." In that role, I was to act as the base commander's representative during the overnight hours (I never knew why they called it "officer of the *day*"). I was peacefully reading a fascinating military manual when "TEN-HUT!" sharply interrupted the last calm I would ever know on that base. Colonel Queeg was escorted into the room with an expression on his face that exuded the ultimate of disgust for the obvious pitiful state of affairs in "HIS" new kingdom. His face was furrowed with deep frown lines revealing a life of misery, and was chiseled into a granite-like grimace that he could intensify by scrunching his dark bushy eyebrows into terrifying arches while simultaneously directing a scalding gaze like a laser-guided missile at any unfortunate victim that tripped his radar. For the next eighteen months everyone on that base, including King Queeg himself, was completely miserable.

My experiences with Colonel Queeg and his bumbling vice commander, the alcoholic Colonel Stillwater (also not real name, but close) could fill the pages of another book. Recalling all of those experiences, however, would drive me into a deep state of depression, so that book will never be written. Just a tale or two here will adequately make my point about living with something close to the *absolute* Negative Authoritarian.

Of course, Colonel Queeg had decided from the outset of our midnight introduction that I was of value to him only as a subject for his experiments in psychological torture. On a daily basis, he would send me written memos demanding a detailed briefing the next morning, complete with flip charts and handouts, on some inane topic—often that was not even my area of responsibility. (He understood little about the organization of the base—except that he was in charge—and was unwilling to consider that anything had even functioned, much less worked perfectly well, before his arrival.) On many occasions, I would work feverishly all night to prepare one of those briefings and show up at the appointed time with reams of handouts and charts underarm, only to have him ask what the hell I was doing there with all that stuff. I was consistently chided in public about things with which I had no connection, loaded with inconsequential extra duties, and ignored when my work was praised by others or when I was honored by entities outside his control.

One way I devised to deal with his abuse was when his weekly staff meetings were called to order. He reveled in waiting outside the door until the stroke of 7:30 a.m., then entering with great pomp and circumstance as his intoxicated vice commander called the room to attention. Of course everyone eagerly jumped to their feet, as they were expected to do. Only I made it a point to always be the *last* one up—but always only by a split second. That way I could privately revel in my own demonstration of contempt for him, but he could not quite catch me at it. I think he knew, and I loved the frustration that little act of mutiny must have caused him.

Of course I was not the sole target of his insanity. At one time or another, practically everyone on the base was the unfortunate and unexpected recipient of his rage, but I seemed to be his favorite plaything. On one occasion Colonel Queeg called the base chaplain and me into his office as the result of a letter that appeared in a national publication that was critical of an action that Colonel Queeg had taken. He had withdrawn the routine privilege that previously had been provided for base personnel to obtain discounted tickets to a local theatre because he objected to the musical "*Hair*" when it came to town. Colonel Queeg demanded that the chaplain and I assume public blame for *his* decision. When we refused, he actually jumped onto his desk and squatted there in a rage, shouting profanities to us at the top of his lungs. Shortly after that incident, I was assigned to a remote tour in Thailand for my last year in the service—one month after the birth of our daughter.

Forgive me if I seem bitter—but Queeg and Stillwater were evil and utterly incompetent, and their Negativity ruined a perfectly good Air Force base and the lives of numerous people. I heard several years later that Colonel Stillwater had been dismissed from the service, and that Queeg actually had been committed to a mental institution. If true, it was sweet justice, but not soon enough.

Government always does the right thing, but only after exhausting every other possible option.
(Winston Churchill)

Use of Authority can quite consciously be Positive or Negative. There are times when a leader knows that a necessary action will be interpreted negatively by a subordinate, such as when correction or discipline is required. Difficult choices often require use of Authority in a Negative manner that will ultimately bring Positive results. Our president and Congress have not exercised this option nearly often enough when it comes to budgets and other legislation. Weak leaders will too often bow to public opinion when a tough decision needs to be made. Reality dictates that actions of Authority will usually fall somewhere along a scale ranging from severely Positive to severely Negative. The astute leader will determine just where on this scale his actions should fall for the most desirable result. Of course Positive actions generally receive the most popular and favorable results, and Negative actions usually cause the most resistance and unfavorable response. It is important for you as a 3-D Leader to know that there is almost always a choice that is under your control.

When everyone is against you, it means that you are absolutely wrong—or absolutely right.
(Albert Guinon, playwright)

The world is one percent good, one percent bad, ninety-eight percent neutral. It can go one way or the other, depending on which side is pushing. This is why what individuals do is important.
(Hans Habe)

How to Be More Charming

It doesn't matter what you do for a living; it's all sales. It's making people feel good about doing business with you. You meet me. My voice is firm and sunny. I'm smiling. A smile is a primal thing, mighty past words.

1. *The first thing I'm going to say is "Thanks for making time for me"(because you don't owe me squat).*
2. *The next thing I'm going to do is ask about you. I'm going to learn about you, and I'm going to learn from you.*
3. *I'm going to make you laugh. (We're) just a planet full of folks—rich and poor alike—all hoping to get treated better than dirt. I can give them that gift. You can too.*

(Scott Raab, quoted in Readers Digest *from an article in* Esquire*)*

You know by now that I am fond of illustrations to make concepts easier to understand. So here is my illustration of the Positive/Negative scale for the Authority dimension:

– **Authority** +

Negative ⬅➡ Positive

(That's so simple I'm almost ashamed to use it.)

Simple diagrams, however, can help you recall a concept on the run, in the heat of battle, or if you just plain have trouble remembering things. The point is to remember that there isn't *just* Authority as a stand-alone concept. There are Positive to Negative degrees of Authority, and you can choose where along the arrow to place your bet, so to speak.

We know that within each dimension there are numerous individual traits, characteristics, and components. Unlike the Nature/Nurture factor where we described a continuum for the *group* of traits, the Positive/Negative continuum applies to *each* trait or characteristic. A list of traits for the **Authority** dimension from chapter 4 is repeated below. Rather than discussing the Positive/Negative factors for each of these examples, I simply ask that you consider for a moment how each of these can have Positive and Negative implications.

Examples of Authority

Power	Assertiveness	Aggressiveness	Determination
Persistence	Leverage	Type of Position	Image
Influence	Confidence	Policies/Procedures	Strength
Stamina	Force	Intelligence	Prestige
Control	Boldness	Autonomy	Dominance
Nobility	Decisiveness	Supervisor's latitude	Command

Positive/Negative Ability

Having studied the effects of Positive and Negative factors on Authority traits, now take a look at the Ability traits in this table:

<u>Examples of Abilities</u>

Intelligence	Timing	Planning	Organizing
Budgeting	Flexibility	Delegating	Teaching
Communication	Public Speaking	Use of Resources	Negotiation
Evaluating	Common Sense	Social Awareness	Interpreting Info.
Use of Technology	Correcting Others	Problem-solving	Anticipation
Innovation	Mathematics	Decision-making	Spatial Thinking
Learning	Reasoning	Adaptability	Resolving Conflict
Clarity	Coping	Task Effectiveness	Initiative

As stated earlier, we will not take the time to demonstrate Positive/Negative factors with each of these examples. You can play around with them as you wish. Let's do look at a diagram of Positive/Negative factors and the overall **Ability** dimension:

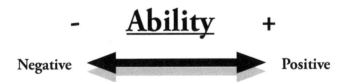

Again, this may seem oversimplified, but let's discuss this concept for a minute. I would say that Positive use of an Ability would be what results in the most good for the most people. For example, Colonel Rogers used his Abilities in a kind and benevolent way that created benefits for his staff, the base or the overall command structure. Colonel Queeg, on the other hand, used his Abilities as a means of making it clear that he was in charge—even if it meant undoing all of the good that Colonel Rogers had accomplished. Colonel Queeg was probably very insecure (in addition to being just plain nuts), and such people *have* to use their Abilities just to reassure themselves. I am quite certain that he clearly chose Negative uses of his Abilities because those actions generated fear in his staff. He believed that fear got the quickest action with the least discussion—which is probably correct. What he did not realize is that while Negative use of Abilities might produce quick results, such results are often only temporary because people are not *committed* to those results. Commitment is achieved through Positive uses of leadership because people identify with the decisions and feel shared ownership—plus they simply *like* the outcomes.

We succeed in enterprises which demand the positive qualities we possess, but we excel in those which can also make use of our defects.
(Alexis de Tocqueville)

A leader's job is to make it easy to do the right thing and difficult to do the wrong thing.
(Bits and Pieces)

One of my favorite examples of Negative use of Abilities appeared on the website *GoUpstate.com* in February 2012. The article says that Jim Preacher arrived in rural Norway, SC twenty years ago. During that time he served as the town's police chief, self-proclaimed constable, and most recently the mayor. As you will see, he has used some heavy-handed tactics, but he is not very apologetic. In a town council meeting, he said, "Somebody has got to take accountability. I was elected, and that's what I am going to do. I may not do it gracefully like a ballerina. I might be more like an elephant in a china shop."

Preacher has never steered clear of controversy. Back when he was a sheriff's deputy in another county, the South Carolina Supreme Court called his work in a murder investigation "reprehensible."

While he served as Norway's police chief he took over the town's waterworks. Shortly after he was fired as police chief he filed a lawsuit against the town claiming they owed him $30,000 for his work with the water system. Still, he was elected mayor beginning in 2012. Preacher didn't want to wait until the monthly council meeting for his formal swearing in, however, so on January 1 he sneaked into the town hall, changed the locks and took over the bank account. The former mayor wanted Preacher arrested, but the state law enforcement division determined there wasn't a break-in because the building was not secured!

Just a few weeks later, a state trooper stopped Preacher, who was driving the town's old police car, for going 70 mph in a 55 mph zone. Preacher claimed that he was the town's constable, and that he was investigating an incident at a convenience store. The trooper knew that the town had disbanded its police department so he issued the ticket anyway. As the patrolman pulled away, Preacher flipped on *his* blue lights and pulled over the trooper, threatening to charge *him* with interfering with a police officer. Even though Preacher decided to drop the matter, he said to the trooper, "Son, you've got a lot to learn," then blasted his siren for three seconds and concluded, "You have a nice night."

State agents said Preacher is no longer certified to be a state constable, but he retorted that he is a *town* constable, and that there is a difference. After an outcry from people in town, he agreed to stop doing police work.

During his first town council meeting as mayor, Preacher asked the former mayor (whom he had defeated by five votes) for her help in getting together the town files. Then he threatened to not allow her to speak again in the meeting and brought up her relationship with another man in town. "He's so power hungry," said the former mayor. "He just wants to be a dictator."

Preacher claimed that he was trying to save the town of Norway, which had fallen on hard times and lost much of its ability to function. Whether justified or not, Preacher would probably agree with the following quote:

> *"Safety first" has been the motto of the human race for half a million years, but has never been the motto of leaders. A leader must face danger. He must take the risk and bear the brunt of the storm.*
> *(Herbert N. Casson, historian)*

Positive/Negative Character

One way to create positive Character is by simple attitude. A woman related an experience in which her father implanted an indelible image of a Positive outlook on her when she was a child. She said that every now and then her mother liked to make breakfast food for dinner. One night in particular after a long, hard day at work the mom placed a plate of eggs, sausage and extremely burned biscuits in front of her husband. All he did was reach for one of those burned biscuits, smile, and ask how the little girl's day was at school. When the mom apologized for burning the biscuits, the dad said, "Baby, I love burned biscuits." That was a simple choice he made that had an immediate Positive impact on his wife, and made a lifelong impression on his daughter. A Positive demonstration of Character is not all that hard to come by, but can make all the difference in the world.

Your Character should probably be the least visible dimension of your leadership. Indeed the *Tree-D Leadership* model in chapter 11

demonstrates this quite clearly. Part of that visibility will depend on the Nature/Nurture factor, and part of it will depend on the choices you make regarding Positive/Negative factors. The important thing to remember is that *you* can make many of the choices.

Now we have learned that all three dimensions—**Authority, Ability, and Character**—can be viewed in terms of Nature/Nurture and Positive/Negative factors. This means that even though some of the traits and components of leadership may be natural or inborn, and some of them may be essentially Positive or essentially Negative, we still have a great deal of control over how we employ them. Just as there are two extremes to Positive/Negative factors, there are two steps to making use of that knowledge: (1) awareness of the options, and (2) choosing an approach.

Reading the Rings

Human beings are marvelously complex, yet are guided by concepts that can be easily applied. Understanding the simple dichotomy of Positive/ Negative factors in relation to your Authority, Abilities, and Character can give you an edge as a leader.

The next time you consciously use one of the dimensions of leadership, visualize the Positive/Negative scale and use that framework to plan your approach.

9

Task/People Factor

In the beginning God created the heavens and the earth. The earth was without form, and void; and darkness was on the face of the deep. And the spirit of God was hovering over the face of the waters.

Then God said, "Let there be light"; and there was light. And God saw the light, that it was good; and God divided the light from the darkness. God called the light Day, and the darkness He called Night. So the evening and the morning were the first day.

—Genesis 1:1–5, NKJV

God, the original Leader of Leaders, found it necessary as His first acts to focus on Tasks rather than People. He was preparing the way for his greatest Creation, man, by using His *Natural* Abilities in a *Positive* manner to perform the *Tasks* of creating the earth, heavens, waters, night and day, grass, seeds, trees, sun and moon, birds and sea creatures, and finally cattle and beasts of the earth before he focused on People.

And then the Bible says:

And on the seventh day God ended his <u>work</u> (emphasis added) *which he had done, and He rested on the seventh day ... (Genesis 2:2a, NKJV)*

And then, for a while at least, God turned His attention to People. He "formed man of the dust of the ground, and breathed into his nostrils the breath of life, and man became a living being." For the rest of time since The Beginning, God has alternated His emphasis between Tasks and People to bring us into the modern world. He created the Garden of Eden, a female companion, the Tree of Life and the serpent, and then banished His beloved human creatures from the Garden for their disobedience. Later He had Noah perform the Task of building the ark to preserve his family (People), then God allowed the Great Flood (Task), once again correcting His children (People) for their wrongdoings (Tasks). Many years later God, through Moses, parted the Red Sea (Task) to allow His People to escape from the Egyptians. And on and on it has gone, including the greatest gift to His People—His own Son, and the worst Task of all—the crucifixion of that Son—for the ultimate salvation of His People. Of course God is not done with us yet, but here we are, facing our own choices of Tasks or People—both of which are necessary at one time or another.

In chapter 3, *"What is Leadership?"* I referred to a favorite old textbook by Paul Hersey and Kenneth Blanchard, *Management of Organizational Behavior: Utilizing Human Resources* (1977). In that book, the authors described how *task behavior* and *relationship behavior* affects a person's leadership style. They defined *task behavior* as explaining "what activities each (follower) is to do and when, where, and how tasks are to be accomplished." *Relationship behavior* was defined as "The extent to which leaders are likely to maintain personal relationships between themselves and members of their group ..."

Over the years, other leadership experts have utilized and adapted this *task/relationship* concept and have used various terms to describe it. I have made my own adaptations, using the terms Task/People factors, and I generally intend for those terms to mean, quite simply:

- Task factor: Use of Authority, Ability, and/or Character traits to focus on actions that accomplish an objective, assignment, function, or other undertaking.

- People factor: Use of Authority, Ability, and/or Character traits to focus on actions that affect People (employees, followers, or members of the leader's group).

> *All of the great leaders have had one characteristic in common: it was the willingness to confront unequivocally the major anxiety of their people in their time. This, and not much else, is the essence of leadership.*
> *(John Kenneth Galbraith)*

> *History keeps her secrets longer than most of us. But she has one secret that I will reveal to you tonight in the greatest confidence. Sometimes there are no winners at all. And sometimes nobody needs to lose.*
> *(John le Carre)*

In almost all cases, whatever goals a leader may set should at some level have the best interests of the *People* at heart. Certainly people like to see their leaders win, succeed, prevail, conquer. Most or all of that success, however, should result in some gains for the group, and certainly must not be at the expense of those whom the leader serves.

David Gergen, in a June 2006 article for *U. S. News & World Report ("Bad News for Bullies," p. 54)* succinctly described this concept. He began with the question "Have you ever worked for a tyrant?" (After reading my description of Colonel Queeg, you will probably agree that *I* certainly have.) Bergen notes that four out of five employees say they have worked for a tyrant at one time or another. My wife and both children (teacher, engineer, and nurse) also claim membership in that group. Surveys also find that the most frequent complaint among all employees is the bully boss. Gergen says, "There are signs that the practice of tormenting employees is rising in the 'new economy,' as companies face stiffer competition and CEO's turn over faster, developing few personal bonds with people around them."

The People's preferred alternative is what Robert K. Greenleaf coined as "the servant leader" in an essay by that title. Greenleaf argues that too many leaders in the past have been driven by a need for power or ambition. (Amen to that!) Today, people are less inclined to blindly accept forceful leadership and prefer instead those who cultivate less coercive relationships. As Gergen points out, Christ taught that in order to lead, one must wash the feet of others, serve each other, that the first will be last, and many who are last will be first.

When you are invited by anyone to a wedding feast, do not sit down in the best place, lest one more honorable than you be invited by him; and he who invited you and him come and say to you, 'Give place to this man,' and then you begin with shame to take the lowest place. But when you are invited, go and sit down in the lowest place, so that when he who invited you comes he may say to you, 'Friend, go up higher.' Then you will have glory in the presence of those who sit at the table with you. For whoever exalts himself will be humbled, and he who humbles himself will be exalted.
(Luke 14: 8–11, NKJV)

In the early days of our country, leaders like George Washington signed their letters, "Your most humble servant." Imagine getting a letter signed like that from *any* elected official today! Gergen notes, however, that few if any leaders could "climb the slippery pole of politics who lacks personal drive and is purely selfless." In today's business and political world, leaders must "have a streak of toughness." He goes on to say that "Increasingly, the best leaders are those who don't order but persuade; don't dictate but draw out; don't squeeze but grow the people around them."

Peter Drucker insists that People in an organization are its number one asset. Max DePree, former chair of Herman Miller Inc. promoted a "covenant" with his employees. He wrote that leaders should give employees "space so that we can both give and receive such beautiful things as ideas, openness, dignity, joy, healing, and inclusion." Gergen concludes his article with the following affirmation of the importance of People in the organization: "Studies show (young professionals are) less interested in power and prestige than in positive relations with colleagues and interesting challenges—the bully may finally see his end."

> A leader is best when people barely know he exists. When his work is done, his aim fulfilled, they will say: We did this ourselves.
> (Lao Tzu, 600 BC–531 BC)

There *are* other ways to deal with bullies. Remember my silent, almost invisible rebellion against Colonel Queeg? I got an unbelievable inner satisfaction at each and every staff meeting knowing that I was the *very last* person to stand up when he entered the room! It was fine if he knew, because there wasn't much he could do about it. It was also okay if he didn't know, because that way I was pulling something over on him!

One of the best methods of "private rebellion" became an Internet sensation several years ago when a man calling himself simply "Ray" recorded a special song for his daughter who was experiencing stress on the job. (I have since discovered that his name is Ray Hagan, and he is, I believe, a minister in St. Louis. The fact that he is a minister, archeologist, regular tour guide to Egypt, and otherwise Renaissance-seeming guy adds to the hilarity of his song.) He introduces the piece by explaining that his daughter called him because she was stressed out about her job, and because it was so unfair. Ray felt a little frustrated himself, since there wasn't really much he could do, so he wrote this song to cheer her up and for the benefit "of all employees under stress." He set it to a catchy, bluesy tune:

Iiiiii'm about to whip somebody's aaaaassss;
Ooh, Iiii'm about to whip somebody's aaasss.
Oh IF you don't leave me alooone, mmm,
You're gonna have to send me home …
'Cause Iiiii'm about to whip somebody's aaaasss!

Ray went on to say, "Now you might not be able to sing that out loud, but you can *hum* it to yourself, and you know what the words are, and let it give you some strength to get through the next few moments on your job."

(My advice to all bosses is to look this song up on the Internet and learn to recognize the tune in case your employees seem to be humming on the job a lot!)

> *Start with where people are before you try to take them to where you want them to go.*
> *(Jim Rohn)*

> *If you don't understand that you work for your mislabeled "subordinates," then you know nothing of leadership.*
> *(Dee Hock, founder of Visa)*

I may need to keep reminding you that there is nothing wrong with focusing on Tasks—indeed such a focus can be quite necessary much of the time. A really good leader can get the Task accomplished, however, by starting out with a People focus. In many ways, focusing on Tasks primarily requires the use of your Ability dimension, whereas an emphasis on People frequently draws from the dimension of Character. Another way to give priority to People is encouraging and supporting *teamwork*. Using teamwork is a version of delegating, although we may initially think of delegating as assigning work or responsibility to an individual. The beauty of delegating to a team is that the whole group has a vested interest in the outcome, as opposed to just one person. Here are some characteristics of a true team:

1. Contains several members, but usually five to ten.
2. Comes together for common goals.
3. Work is shared and delegated.
4. Individual and group effort seems to maximize human effort.
5. An emotional sense of commitment to objectives exists, as well as a sense of urgency for action and accomplishment.
6. Reaches decisions on the basis of consensus.

> *Good leadership requires you to surround yourself with people of diverse perspectives who can disagree with you without fear of retaliation.*
> *(Doris Kearns Goodwin)*

Delegating to *individuals* as well as teams also works wonders for helping employees feel empowered and engaged. (You just usually get more bang for the buck by spreading the work among several people.) Remember, however, the old adage that you cannot delegate *responsibility* without also delegating *authority*. It's not fair to expect someone (or a team) to be responsible for something if they can't make decisions and commitments to make it happen. On the other hand, you cannot delegate *all* of the responsibility, you can only *share it*. If you are responsible for something, delegating does not *relieve* you of that responsibility.

Delegating work works, provided the one delegating works, too.
(Robert Half)

Placing a huge emphasis on a special Task can also be a great way to fundamentally focus on the People of the organization. In other words, if you frame the Task in such a way that it *motivates* the People, then you have effectively married Task and People. Great leaders have often clearly defined the Task, set a lofty yet feasible timetable, and then let the People run with it. Television correspondent Charles Osgood called it "setting an agenda" and referred to John F. Kennedy's call in the early 1960s for America to put a man on the moon by the end of the decade. Osgood said, "There were lots of problems that would have to be solved— technical, political, and money problems—but Kennedy didn't try to solve them all in advance. All he did was set a definite timetable. He left it to others to work out how it was going to be done." And as we all know, Neil Armstrong took his "giant leap for mankind" on the surface of the moon July 21,1969.

Goals are dreams with deadlines.
(Diana Scharf Hunt)

Clearly setting and understanding goals, objectives, strategies, and deadlines are vital steps to a Task-oriented approach, even for less lofty agendas than moon landings. Taking things for granted is a common mistake, both among employees and supervisors. A supervisor may tell her employees that she expects sales to increase by 10 percent. Everybody agrees, except that some may work feverishly to increase sales beginning today for the rest of all time, and some may wait until the end of the month to get 10 percent more just for that month, then lapse back to the original level for the rest of all time! There's a story about a famous Mexican general who could please everyone by simply saying "yes" (or "si" I suppose) to all requests; he just never said *when*.

A wonderful little book called *The One Minute Manager* by Ken Blanchard and Spencer Johnson promotes the simple yet profound practices of One-Minute Goals, One-Minute Praisings, and One-Minute Reprimands. Too many supervisors wait until annual performance evaluations to give this kind of direction and feedback to their employees (or never give it at all). Impromptu on-the-spot praise, especially, can mean a great deal to an employee for many reasons. I worked for two college presidents whose handwritten notes of thanks and praise flowed like a fountain, and the employees and students who received them responded by excelling further in their work.

A human being has a need for dignity, just like water, like air.
(Wole Soyinka)

It takes discipline and perseverance to make writing thank-you notes a regular part of a leader's routine, but such a practice can completely reshape the image of that leader in the eyes of others. An issue of Ragan Publication's *"Employee Recruitment & Retention"* periodical several years ago promoted the idea of being *specific* in your praise, as general "great job" comments get worn out quickly. The publication gave these suggestions for "openers" to help supervisors with specificity:

- "You really made a difference by ..."
- "I'm impressed with ..."
- "You got my attention with ..."
- "You're doing top quality work on ..."
- "You're right on the mark with ..."
- "You can be proud of yourself for ..."
- "What an effective way to ..."
- "You've made my day because of ..."

Retreats and in-service training can provide excellent balance for Task and People perspectives. One exercise that I especially liked involved using Tinker Toys to identify and develop leadership skills. Several small groups were provided with sets of Tinker Toys and instructed to see which group could build the "best" tower within a certain time limit, with the restriction that no one could talk. This process is rich in a variety of leadership challenges. The exercise consistently demonstrates the three Dimensions of Leadership and the Task/People factor:

1. Someone assumes or is given **Authority** (a leader) by the other members (**People**) to accomplish the **Task.**
2. The leader and members of the group (**People**) use their **Abilities** to make the tower as structurally sound and as tall as possible within the time limit(**Task**).
3. The group (**People**) is called upon to use imagination, creativity, integrity and a host of other **Character** traits to build (**Task**) a high-quality design without breaking the rules, and they also have a lot of fun in the process.

When we turn to one another for counsel we reduce the number of our enemies. (Kahlil Gibran, 1883–1931, poet and novelist)

Leadership simply does not happen without the dynamics of focusing alternatively between **Task** and **People** factors.

The first task of a leader is to keep hope alive. (Joe Batten)

Leaders have two important characteristics: First, they're going somewhere; second, they're able to persuade other people to go along with them. (Bits and Pieces magazine)

But also don't forget Nature/Nurture and Positive/Negative factors. (You may be beginning to think that this whole concept of 3-D Leadership is getting a little too complicated. I encourage you, however, to focus on the broad principles and how they easily fit together.) My model of 3-D Leadership is intended to make leadership simultaneously simple and comprehensive by providing visual images that help you "wrap your arms around" the whole thing. Spend a little time "Reading the Rings" below to help pull together everything you have learned so far.

Reading the Rings

Think of the three Dimensions of Leadership
with each having
three factors to consider:

N/N = Nature/Nurture
P/N = Positive/Negative
T/P = Task/People

Dimensions	Factors
Authority	N/N P/N T/P
Ability	N/N P/N T/P
Character	N/N P/N T/P

3 Dimensions. Each has
the same 3 Factors. Simple, isn't it?

_Coach Bear Bryant
was always fair. He
treated every one
of us like trash.—
(ForrestGump)_

10

The Three Perspectives of a Leader

The Three Perspectives of a Leader

Mirror, mirror, on the wall—who's the fairest of them all? The answer to that, my friends, depends on your Perspective. There are three impressions to consider:

- the person that *you* think you are;
- the person that *others* think you are;
- and the *real* person that is you.

Those three Perspectives can be very nearly the same, or they can be wildly different. Effective leadership involves understanding and managing the differences between *your* Perspective, *their* Perspective, and the *real* Perspective. Let's make sure we understand first what is meant by Perspective. Quite in line with the theme of this chapter is the fact that there is a *dictionary* definition and *my* definition. Dictionary.com indicates eight definitions of perspective, three of which closely suit my purpose, but not quite:

1. The state of one's ideas, the facts known to one, etc., in having a meaningful interrelationship.

2. The faculty of seeing all the relevant data in a meaningful relationship.
3. A mental view or prospect.

My Perspective on the word Perspective combines the three official versions above, with just a tiny tweak or two. The result is this personal definition:

Perspective: *A mental view or prospect that uses relevant data and known facts to reflect the state of one's ideas.* So here is my best attempt at graphically depicting the three Perspectives of Leadership:

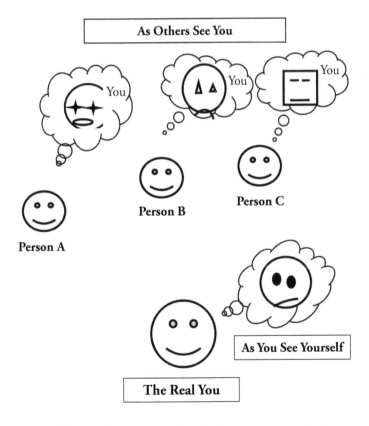

The problem, of course, is that the Perspectives of others and of yourself are never quite accurate—they never quite match the Real

You. Those Perspectives are influenced by all sorts of factors, some of which are firmly fixed and others which fluctuate based on the circumstances. These factors include such things as

- what others *want* to see,
- their attitude at the time,
- *your* attitude,
- timing of events,
- the physical environment (is it simply too hot in the room while you are giving a speech?),
- your physical appearance,
- and numerous other factors—I'm sure you can come up with a few of your own.

Your challenge, especially as a leader, is to understand those Perspectives—and where possible try to influence them to more accurately reflect the Real You. (Many unscrupulous leaders, of course, would much rather manipulate their image *away from* reality.)

You can apply this Perspective concept to understand yourself better, but you can also use it to evaluate other leaders, such as those running for office in your school organization, people you are considering for promotion in your company, or politicians running for public office.

Every man is a moon and has a [dark] side which he turns toward nobody; you have to slip around behind if you want to see it.
(Mark Twain)

To each, his own ca-ca smells sweet—but do not be fooled by this.
(Forrest Gump)

Perspective can apply to a person as a whole, or to each of that person's three Dimensions of Leadership (**Authority, Ability,** and **Character**). In other words, you can have *your own* Perspective about a leader's Authority, and that leader will have *his own* Perspective of his Authority, while there is a *real* Authority dimension for that person that may be different from your view or his own view. The same goes for the other dimensions of Ability and Character. As I have said before, this may begin to sound a bit complicated, but it's not, really. Keep in mind the visual models—and when we get into the Tree model in the next chapter you will find it even easier to visualize all of the concepts presented up to this point.

I have emphasized that it is possible to *manage* Perspectives to some degree. It is also important to know when to adjust Perspective and when to leave it alone. An ancient Egyptian concept known as *Maat* (pronounced *Ma-at*) recognizes that there is a certain order to the universe based on truth, balance, law, morality, and justice. According to Wikipedia, Maat embraces all aspects of existence, including the basic equilibrium of the universe, the relationship between constituent parts, the cycle of the seasons, and other universal concepts. Any disturbance in the cosmic harmony could have consequences for the individual as well as the state. Maat can be summed up one way by saying "Be what you are." An example might be seen in the fact that birds are birds—but eagles don't hang out with sparrows, and cranes don't socialize with crows—yet they are all *birds* and know that they belong to that order of the universe.

Don't be no Ant-Man. An Ant-Man has very low horizons. (Forrest Gump)

Part of the challenge for effective leadership is living with this delicate balance between accepting Perspective and managing Perspective. The following diagram appeared in an email I received from a friend. I thought it was a pretty easy way to visualize Perspective:

Success

What people think it looks like   *What it really looks like*

Now take a glance at the following:

No matter what anyone says,

You
are
never
stupid!

Your first impression of the above sentence may have been from the wrong Perspective. This can be a lesson that we can apply to life in general—don't always assume that your first impression is the *real* impression; sometimes you need to take a closer look, or listen more carefully, or consider what motivation the other person really had.

Several years ago, I taught a graduate-level course in public school administration that met one night each week. The students were mostly public school teachers who were working on their master's degrees, with the objective of advancing into leadership positions. One of the techniques I used was engaging the students in formal debates, where teams represented the affirmative and negative arguments relating to a particular question. A question to be debated might be something like "Should public schools require students to wear uniforms?" The affirmative team would do research and argue in favor of uniforms and the negative team would present arguments opposed to uniforms. The week before the first debate I explained the process and assigned specific students to affirmative and negative teams. One student—let's call her Sherry—who had been assigned to the negative team missed class the week of the debate. When time came during the process for Sherry's turn to present research opposing school uniforms, I simply asked any student in the audience if they would like to use Sherry's time to make points supporting the negative team's argument. The next week Sherry wasn't present, and I later learned that she had unexpectedly withdrawn from the class.

Another student told me that Sherry had quit because I had embarrassed her with my comments during the debate. When I called to ask her about the withdrawal, Sherry explained that another student who had taken notes for her in her absence wrote that "Since you weren't here, Dr. Hartzog just allowed anyone to make negative comments." Sherry thought it was awful that I would allow students to make negative comments about her just because she was absent! It took me a long time to convince Sherry the *real* Perspective about those comments. Even though she *said* she understood, she never did return to the class. (That incident bothered me for years, because one of the most frustrating things in life for me is *being misunderstood*.)

Perhaps sharks can truly demonstrate perspective in adapting to their environment. According to John Maxwell in *A Leader's Heart*, "One popular aquarium fish is the shark. The reason is that sharks adapt to their environment. If you catch a small shark and confine it, it will stay a size proportionate to the aquarium in which it lives. Sharks can be six inches long yet fully mature. But if you turn them loose in the ocean, they grow to their normal size." (I can't find any scientific evidence to support or refute this, but it is certainly an amazing thought!)

Mountains appear more lofty the nearer they are approached, but great leaders resemble them not in this particular.
(Lady Marguerite Blessington, Irish writer)

I think the important point here is that as a leader you should seek the *most effective you* and not necessarily make continuous comparisons with others. What is effective for one person may be entirely inappropriate for another. Early in life, I developed decent skills in public speaking (among other things, I won the South Carolina American Legion High School Oratorical Contest and received the highest ratings in numerous other speech contests). And I have always loved a good joke. So I confidently auditioned once to be the emcee at a talent show for an Air Force ROTC summer camp, attempting to imitate famous people telling jokes. Bad mistake. Somehow, my public speaking abilities and joke-telling just did not result in the dynamite performer I thought I could be. The planners of the show were polite, but my ego was deflated when they selected someone else to be the emcee. I later realized how embarrassing it would have been to fall flat in front of five hundred of my peers instead of just the two officers who saw the *real* me, and let me down gently!

Don't undermine your worth by comparing yourself with others. It is because we are different that each of us is special.
(Brian Dyson)

Several experiences like the emcee audition taught me that what is *inside* is usually the most important factor in life. You can be depressed by failure or rejection, or you can change your Perspective, adapt, and move on.

But the Lord said to Samuel, "Do not look at his appearance or at his physical stature, because I have refused him. For the Lord does not see as man sees; for man looks at the outward appearance, but the Lord looks at the heart.
(1 Samuel 16:7)

Be more concerned with your character than with your reputation. Your character is what you really are, while your reputation is merely what others think you are.
(John Wooden)

Sometimes only a change of viewpoint is needed to convert a tiresome duty into an interesting opportunity.
(Alberta Flanders)

Vision is vital to effective leadership. We listed this term in the examples of Character traits in chapter 6, but vision is also instrumental in determining Perspective. There are several ways to consider vision as a Perspective factor. Vision can refer to the grand scheme of life, of the ultimate purpose of your organization, or in a more restricted sense, of how you view yourself and others. For any of these interpretations it matters greatly what your vantage point is for your vision, and how you express it.

Usually you have a choice in setting up your vantage point, but not always. For example, we can and should consider the needs and desires of the organization when determining a vision for the group. On the other hand, we may have to do research and learn about the history of our school club, or the governmental district that we have been elected to represent. And sometimes we are unexpectedly faced with choices to make relying solely on our admittedly limited perspective.

It helps to look as far down the road as possible, because leaders do more than control the direction in which they and their people travel. They must see the whole trip in their minds. According to John Maxwell, a leader sees …

- *Farther than others see.*
- *More than others see.*
- *Before others see.*

Prepare as best you can, but when the time comes, you must present your vision as clearly and as confidently as possible.

> *You have to have a vision. It's got to be a vision you articulate clearly and forcefully. You can't blow an uncertain trumpet.*
> *(Rev. Theodore Hesburgh)*

> *For if the trumpet makes an uncertain sound, who will prepare for battle?*
> *(1 Corinthians 14:8)*

While it is important not to blow an uncertain trumpet, that doesn't mean you have to blow their socks off either. There is always something to be said for the still, small voice that gets attention amid chaos and confusion. I have observed many teachers—especially elementary school teachers—who can get the attention of a rowdy classroom simply by almost whispering instructions to the class. The focus of the students immediately changes from dealing with each other to listening to the teacher. Their Perspective shifts and the teacher regains her leadership role. How you speak helps determine how other people see you as a leader. We have all seen effective speakers alternate from fever-pitch highs to a sudden hushed moment with an almost whispered point that entrances the audience.

> *It makes you look good when you avoid a fight.*
> *(Proverbs 20:3)*

> *Even fools seem smart when they are quiet.*
> *(Proverbs 17:28)*

One of the real difficulties of working with Perspectives is that they are often moving targets. People may see you one way today and think of you differently tomorrow. You can be convinced that a candidate for public office has been an idiot since birth, yet discover one day that she was not the person you thought she was. It is difficult to know sometimes whether what you are seeing or hearing is the real deal or if there may be something behind it that is unseen and unheard.

> *Never accept "no." Things change—in the environment, people's perceptions, and the situation—so always seek the angles that move you toward your goal.*
> *(Rose Marie Bravo)*

Then there is the matter of Perspectives changing reality. Weak leaders find it extremely tempting to go along with the crowd—or to do whatever is popular, convenient, or feels good at the time. Remember the *real* you, that core of who you are that is true to the principle of *Maat*. Remaining true to your core values is a matter of integrity, which is one of the key Character traits. Some leaders seem to ride waves of popularity like a surfer, always choosing just the right swell to place them high above the surrounding sea. They ride those waves until they are completely played out, and then find the next wave to take advantage of. The problem is that waves are not permanent—they have no foundation, and they last only a little while. Eventually the sea becomes calm and there are no waves to ride—and the surfer comes crashing down to reality, left paddling aimlessly, hoping for another wave.

Keen awareness of the three Perspectives—

- how you see yourself,
- how others see you,
- and the real you—

can prepare you for the challenges of leadership, for the waxing and waning of popular opinion and can help hone your vision so that you can see *farther than others see, more than others see, and before others see.*

A man of honor should never forget what he is because he sees what others are.
(Baltasar Gracian)

Reading the Rings

The next time you see a national leader on television, visualize the cartoon-like images on page 121 that represent the three Perspectives.

Who does he think he is?
Who do you think he is?
What is he really like if you "go around to the other side"?

11

The Tree-Dimensional Model

I think that I shall never see
A poem lovely as a tree.

A tree whose hungry mouth is prest
Against the sweet earth's flowing breast;

A tree that looks at God all day,
And lifts her leafy arms to pray;

A tree that may in summer wear
A nest of robins in her hair;

Upon whose bosom snow has lain;
Who intimately lives with rain.

Poems are made by fools like me,
But only God can make a tree.

—Joyce Kilmer, 1919

Photo by Author, Blue Ridge Parkway

I had forgotten how brief and beautiful this poem is. My general recollection was of lengthy, flowing verses describing all sorts of

131

trees, but the real thing is so much better than my memory portrayed (this demonstrates the point of the previous chapter about varying Perspectives)!

Trees are everywhere, and they are all beautiful creations of God. Some, however, appeal to us for certain purposes while others do not. In nature, trees grow in practically every possible environment; they adapt, taking on an amazing variety of shapes, sizes, and colors; some bear fruit, some provide bountiful shade, some hide nests for birds, some have knotholes for squirrels, some are used to build houses, some are crafted into intricate carvings, and some even make strange sounds!

David Mabberley, in his foreword to the visual reference guide *Trees* (2010) masterfully describes the universal role of these handiworks of God:

In every society, trees provide food in the form of fruits and nuts, flavorings, and even edible flowers and leaves. Trees are the source of pharmaceuticals, as well as building timber and firewood. Their protective bark provides not only medicines but also resins, barkcloth, and cork. Their heartwood and water-transport systems produce long-lasting wood that is used to make furniture and the pulp for all modern books and newspapers. Trees provide the bases for the perfume industry.

As a whole, forests harbor 75 percent of the world's biodiversity. Trees intercept rainfall and gently release it in watersheds; they absorb carbon dioxide and replenish the air with oxygen. Trees are planted to restore degraded landscapes and provide forage for hungry animals. They protect coastlines and riverbanks. Some act as important shade trees and windbreaks; many others are grown as ornamentals.

The original vegetation of much of the world was dominated by trees, and our ancestors were tree-living primates. Trees were the sources of food and medicine long before there was human consciousness. They still feature strongly in our human psyche: the forbidding forests of fairy tales, sacred groves, the Tree of Knowledge, and the Tree of Life—in Christianity, Jesus's cross is often called "the Tree." We have a great fascination with the tallest and oldest trees, which span generations of human lives. Their majestic gigantism is as attractive as that of the dinosaurs.

In our landscaping, we select trees for size, color, leaf type, hardiness, insect and disease resistance, size of root systems, type of fruit or nuts, ease of maintenance and many other characteristics.

If only we devoted the same amount of care and attention to choosing and nurturing Leadership—our own leadership qualities and those of leaders we vote for, hire, train and depend on! Here is part of the answer:

Tree-Dimensional Leadership

Buried within this image of a noble tree is all that you need to know about Leadership. Really. The effective content of 503 million documents and 216 million books on leadership, all right there in one image of a tree in which you can sense Height, Width and Depth.

Authority.
Ability.
Character.
(This is Leadership, plain and simple.)

In this concept of using trees to represent the world of Leadership, the fundamental thought process is to associate the trunk of a tree with Authority, the branches with Abilities, and the roots as Character.

It is difficult not to think of trees in anthropomorphic terms; no wonder people hug them, for the human pattern of slow maturity but long productivity is strangely analogous.
(Alan Paterson, in Best Trees for Your Garden)

The poem *"Scrubb"* by Edna St. Vincent Millay reads almost as a *contrapositive* to the pleasantry and beauty of the classic by Kilmer that was quoted at the beginning of this chapter:

If I grow bitterly,
Like a gnarled and stunted tree, ...
If I make of my drawn boughs
An Inhospitable House ...
It is that a wind too strong
Beat my back when I was young,
It is that I fear the rain
Lest it blister me again."

Background: www.123rf.com

Even these two beautifully-stated poems with oblique Perspectives can demonstrate the relevance of trees as images of leadership. Some leaders are strengthened and nourished by storms, rain and age, while others are misshapen, weakened and even uprooted by the realities of the world.

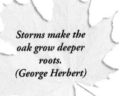

Storms make the oak grow deeper roots.
(George Herbert)

https://t.co/m8gAgTBAmq

It is my hope that after reading this book, you will always associate trees and leadership, so that you will be frequently reminded of the importance and functions of Authority, Ability, and Character. When you observe various types of tree trunks, branches and roots, you will constantly be reinforcing your knowledge of effective leadership. I often find myself amazed at the general variety of trees, and how so many of them remind me of leaders that I know. It helps me to "size up" leaders by visualizing them as types of trees, and conversely, when I see a tree with a notable shape I try to think what leader or type of leader that tree represents.

And all the trees of the field shall know that I the Lord have brought down the high tree, have exalted the low tree, have dried up the green tree, and have made the dry tree to flourish: I the Lord have spoken and have done it.
(Ezekiel 17:24, KJV)

Let's explore the concept of Tree-Dimensional Leadership by examining how special characteristics of trees represent the dimensions and interrelationships of leadership traits. You will remember that I began this book with the concept of "3-D Leadership," using a box or cube as the model.

Certainly trees are far more interesting, complex and beautiful:

Photo by author, Milliken Arboretum, Spartanburg, SC

The variety of trees in the world is essentially limitless. You might even find that your back yard has examples with unusual characteristics. Life would not exist without trees, for they provide some things we absolutely need, like oxygen, and some things that we just enjoy, like shade and beauty. I'm not sure that life could exist without leaders either. You can ponder on that for a while.

My purpose here is to expand your concept from 3-D Leadership to *Tree*-Dimensional Leadership. After the "big picture" of a forest with all sorts of trees represented above, now visualize a stately (or noble) tree as representing the ideal leader. An actual tree is three-dimensional like everything in nature, having height, width and depth—spreading out in all directions. Just for fun, pull out your red and blue glasses and take a look at the 3-D effect of this noble tree:

www.3amblue.com

The 3-D photo above doesn't provide the complete image that I want you to embrace because it doesn't show a whole tree—branches, roots and all. But it is a neat 3-D effect. So let me bring you back to the "whole" tree concept with this image:

While not exact, you can get a sense of the 16:9 ratio that I first talked about in chapter 1. For purposes of Tree-Dimensional Leadership, this is an ideally-proportioned tree. The image that you would see above ground—the trunk and branches—has more width than height. With the trunk representing Authority, the branches Abilities, and the roots Character, this translates into the ideal leader exhibiting more Abilities and Character than Authority.

I have acknowledged before that no model is perfect, so let me tweak your thinking just a little in regards to applying the 3-D concept to the Tree-Dimensional model: While I do want you to think of the tree model as truly three-dimensional, I need for you to consider the *roots* as the third dimension of depth—not exactly as back-to-front depth, but depth in the sense of "underground depth" and not always being visible. In a way, the tree model is a two-dimensional representation of a three-dimensional concept. This is a tough concept to explain, so I hope you get it!

So now let me take you through a few more steps to convert your mental image of 3-D Leadership to the ***Tree-Dimensional*** model. In chapter 1 you learned about several **Dimensional Properties**. These properties apply just as well to the tree model as they do to the box model:

1. **The only measure of height, width or depth is the distance from one point of that dimension to the other.** *Adapted just a little for the Tree-Dimensional Leadership model, the measure of Authority is the height (and width) of the trunk; the measure of Abilities is the width (and height) of the branches; and the measure of Character is the depth (and width) of the roots.*

2. **There is no limit to the dimensions.** *Who is to say how tall a tree can grow, or how much Authority a leader can have? How wide can the branches extend, or how many can there be? Abilities can be more extensive than we may imagine. Roots can grow to whatever depth they need to anchor a tree or to find moisture. The limits of Character cannot be defined.*

3. **Higher, wider or deeper is not necessarily better.** *Some trees function better with very tall trunks while others require only shallow roots. Landscaping may require branches that can support swings or wispy ones that look good beside a*

pond. Different situations may require different measures of Authority, Abilities, and Character. (I hasten to emphasize here the following Property.)

4. **Width and height are most effectively and pleasantly illustrated when width is greater than height (16:9).** *In general, the most beautiful trees are those with copious symmetrical branches, strong but medium-height trunks, and deep, strong root systems. Certainly other types have their places and functions. Like noble trees, however, good leaders generally maintain the "16:9 ratio" by emphasizing their Abilities and Character more than their Authority.*

5. **Any of the dimensions can be changed without affecting the other dimensions.** *The trunk of a tree can grow to an extended height while its branches and roots remain the same. A leader can increase his Abilities without changing the level of his Authority or the depth of his Character.*

6. **Changes can be made to one, two or all three dimensions.** *Branches, trunks, or root systems can be altered singly or in any combination. Leaders can increase, improve, or even diminish any or all of their dimensions as desired or as necessary.*

7. **Variations of height, width or depth can significantly affect the appearance of an object.** *The shape of trees can be altered quite noticeably by modifications to their limbs, trunks or roots. The image of a leader can be transformed by a change in her Character, Authority, or Abilities.*

Trees are dynamic. They are constantly undergoing change. Most are affected by the seasons, but as the seasons come and go, they also may be growing, temporarily stagnant, or in decline. They can be affected by a lack of nutrients, too much or too little moisture, pests, disease, and human intervention.

Some people walk in the rain. Others just get wet.
(Roger Miller)

Leaders are subject to the same kinds of influences in human terms. They experience the spring years of youth, the summers of full adulthood, the autumns of senior maturity and the winters of declining vigor and influence. Some leaders grow, many become stagnant, and a few wither away. Those who need constant strokes from their followers won't always be fulfilled; some will be weakened by pests that take advantage of their power and influence; others might become infected with diseases such as complacency, overconfidence, callousness, or narcissism. Leaders need constant care, nourishment, and even occasional pruning! They can serve long and well with proper attention to the things that really count.

One must pass through the circumference of time before arriving at the center of opportunity.
(Baltasar Gracian)

I look forward to growing old and wise and audacious.
(Glenda Jackson)

It's easier to have the vigor of youth when you're old than the wisdom of age when you're young.
(Richard J. Needham)

In a sense, I consider this chapter as the apex of the book, where we take a "leap of faith" from basic 3-D Leadership to Tree-Dimensional Leadership, moving from drawings of boxes and lines to represent leadership to the use of living, vibrant trees as images of leadership. In doing so, I have begun to "loop back" to the beginning of the book and revisit the major points, applying them to the tree concept so that you will be able to fully embrace the idea of Tree-Dimensional Leadership.

Hopefully with you barely noticing it, I have already reconnected you with the principles of chapters 1 through 6:

1. *A Basic Explanation of Three Dimensions*
2. *Some Fun Examples of 3-D Magic*
3. *What Is Leadership?*
4. *Authority Represented by Height*
5. *Ability Represented by Width*
6. *Character Represented by Depth*

Now let's continue this trip down memory lane ...

Photo by Author, Milliken Arboretum

...by addressing the principles of chapters 7–10 with the noble tree as the model of Leadership (with a capital L):

7. *Nature/Nurture Factor*
8. *Positive/Negative Factor*
9. *Task/People Factor*
10. *The Three Perspectives of a Leader*

Nature/Nurture Factor

You might remember from chapter 7 that I said the individual traits within each of the three Dimensions of Leadership can be placed somewhere along a continuum from Nature to Nurture. On the Nature end, factors are inborn or granted and on the Nurture end factors are learned, earned or otherwise gained by effort. Trees provide the ultimate evidence of the influences of Nature and Nurture.

> ... *Trees make or at least strongly influence the climate in which they themselves—along with the rest of us—flourish. (Allen Paterson, in Best Trees for Your Garden)*

Allen Paterson, in his book *Best Trees for Your Garden* (2003), unknowingly provides some wonderful material that parallels the concept of trees as images of Leadership. Consider the following quotes from pages 15 through 23 of that book *(with my own comments in italics and enclosed in brackets)*:

> *[To be considered a tree]* a plant needs to develop a framework of permanent woodiness *[trunk and branches—Authority and Abilities]* above the surrounding plant growth. ... Shrubs and ultimately trees ... have exchanged the convenience of continual renewal for dominance of height and hence vital light. *[Height, of course, being synonymous with Authority, which provides dominance.]*
>
> ...the knowledge of origin (is) so important if they are to be successfully grown in cultivation continents away from their homes. *[The most effective leaders are true to their origins. We must also be aware of those origins in order to better understand them.]*

But as most plants don't grow in an environmentally controlled greenhouse protected from the vagaries of climate and terrain, each species has evolved to succeed in a particular ecological niche; it has adapted its form to function and to capitalize on what is available. *[An effective leader in one setting can become quite ineffective when attempting to serve outside his/her familiar environment. If "transplantation" becomes necessary, the leader must adapt and capitalize on available resources.]*

Each (tree), we must accept, is perfect for its role and exquisitely adapted to its environment, yet to us they appear to share identical conditions. It is this that provides much of the fascination that trees hold for us—endless variations on a theme. *[Indeed, while leaders may appear to share the same conditions, their styles or effectiveness will vary infinitely, just as trees do.]*

We can ameliorate the conditions in which we grow plants—improve the soil, add nutrients, irrigate, protect, we can even move somewhere else—but ultimately we are constrained by climate. This is especially the case in growing trees; (while we can construct artificial environments) their enclosure in buildings deprives them of their essential "treeness." *[We can derive two parallels here: First, that leaders can improve their traits and strengths through conscious effort—education, training, and the like, but certain characteristics will remain constant. Second, that a leader may seek a different environment in order to be more effective, but the constraints of his origins go with him.]*

What is truly astonishing about trees is their ability to distribute ... required nutrients to the farthest parts of the organism. If one accepts that the root system below ground is almost a mirror image of what we see stretching a couple of hundred feet up toward the sky, it becomes possible to realize what a miracle of perfect plumbing this is. *[In the same way, our Character traits feed and sustain everything in the other two dimensions of Authority and Abilities. Flaws in Authority or Abilities often may be caused by flaws in Character.]*

… As it can be proved that, aerodynamically, bumblebees cannot fly, so trees have no right to be 300 feet high. *[Remember **Dimensional Property 2:** There is no limit to the Dimensions? Leaders can surprise others—and themselves—by the levels of Authority or other Dimensions they can attain.]*

Tree seedlings … either … can accept a lot of shade, … or they have to wait until a forest giant crashes to the ground, often taking other trees with it, and a glade opens up. There is then a sort of botanical feeding frenzy as plants rush in to capitalize upon the opportunity, until the status quo returns and a new tree canopy shades out the rest.… The rotting trunks of fallen trees act as nurses to their successors, seeds germinating on the rich remains of each corpse, and one finds a straight line of young trees occurring as if planted by a forester. *[I find this passage to be a chillingly accurate portrayal of what happens when succession to leadership positions occurs. Beautiful, and maybe a little grisly at the same time.]*

In most cases of successful leadership, the leaders have been planted in the right spot at the right time—nature has its say—and then they are nourished and tended, while adding layers of Authority, extending and shaping their Abilities and developing deep roots of

Character over time. Just as noble trees can't be rushed to maturity, great leaders must have the natural potential and then develop that potential attentively, judiciously, and prudently.

It takes an oak tree 20 to 50 years to produce its first acorn.

The biggest oak was once just a nut that held its ground. (Sign in a store)

Study this one image of a tree and let your imagination run wild about the effects of Nature/Nurture on the leadership dimensions of Authority (trunk), Abilities (branches), and Character (roots):

Photograph by Author

How did this tree arrive at this stage of growth and shape?

Positive/Negative Factor

Photo by Author

Just as with people (and leaders especially), trees can make a positive or negative image on us. What is your impression of this one? Rather stark, for sure. Dead, probably. Decent Authority (trunk) at one time, but few Abilities (branches), and the roots (Character) are probably all dried up. It's called "The Hanging Tree" at Ghost Town in the Sky at Maggie Valley, NC. That should secure its impression as a negative image in your mind. Still, some good can be seen in just about everything, and you never know what a leader may have been through to arrive at his state of mind.

A mighty wind blew night and day.
It stole the oak tree's leaves away,
Then snapped its boughs and pulled its bark
Until the oak was tired and stark.
But still the oak tree held its ground
While other trees fell all around.
(Hallmark card)

146

People, of course, can be complex. A leader can exhibit Negative or Positive factors in any or all three Dimensions. An all-Negative example may be a leader who is aggressive (Negative Authority), has bad timing (Negative Ability), and is dishonest (Negative Character). Or in any given situation, a leader may exhibit some Positive and some Negative factors: collaborative (Positive Authority), but with faulty reasoning (Negative Ability), and a terrible sense of humor (Negative Character). When a particular leader exhibits Positive and/or Negative factors, visualizing that leader as a tree with matching traits can help you understand that person.

Task/People Factor

Certainly people expect their leaders to see that tasks are accomplished. They also expect to be included. Moses, one of God's foremost examples of leadership, often turned to his people to ensure that tasks were accomplished. The following analysis from *The Word in Life Study Bible* is quite instructive (*The Word in Life Study Bible*, copyright © 1993, 1996 by Thomas Nelson, Inc.):

1. *Moses, himself a man of authority, respected the authority of Jethro.* When Moses became overwhelmed with work to be done, his father-in-law Jethro came to offer advice. Appoint well-qualified men to take on the burden of judging routine matters—you cannot do it all, he said (Exodus 18:13–23). Rather than becoming defensive and defending his turf, Moses listened and responded willingly.
2. *Authority has a way of becoming intoxicating.* This is why so many leaders resist letting others share in the work to be done.
3. *Authority should be invested in others prudently.* Jethro described job qualifications based on proven Character, demonstrating that delegation is a privilege, not a right. A leader ought to consider the quality (Character) and Ability of prospective appointees.
4. *Authority is a resource to be invested in others.* By delegating Authority to subordinates, Moses energized his people to go much further than if he retained total control.

> *Authority is a resource to be used up in empowering others to act more effectively.*
> *(The Word in Life Study Bible)*

5. *Effective leadership increases the health and longevity of an organization and its people.* Organizations are not as effective if only a handful of its members are involved. By giving more members a stake in the outcome, leaders can bring far more eyes, ears, brains, and hands to bear on complex decisions.

Moses and his wise group of judges can be represented as this grove of grand old trees:

Photograph by Author

The prophet Nehemiah also demonstrated the value of focusing on People as well as Tasks. *The Word in Life Study Bible* also provides this background:

When the Jews returned to Jerusalem in the fifth century BC after the Babylonian exile, the city lay in ruins; 152 years earlier, King Nebuchadnezzar had knocked down the walls and burned the city's gates. Now, even though the temple and other parts of the city were being restored, the people did not feel safe without walls around the city. Enter Nehemiah, a prophet and cupbearer to the king. He could have chosen any number of projects to help restore the city, but he chose to rebuild the wall. Why? Because (1) the Task was achievable, (2) the Task was something in which everyone could participate, and (3) the Task had both practical and symbolic value to its People!

When Donald Trump was campaigning for president, I think he sensed this concept by promising to build a wall. It didn't really matter whether it was going to be a big physical wall all the way across the border, or whether Mexico was actually going to pay for it! It mattered to the voters largely in a symbolic sense. And they responded by electing him as their leader to make them feel safe.

Many people regard leadership primarily as the art of getting results. It doesn't matter how. But the great leaders of Scripture like Nehemiah not only accomplished much but served *People* in the process. In fact, his task of rebuilding the wall of Jerusalem was never an end in itself. His ultimate objective was to revitalize the People of Israel and to restore them to their covenant with God.

Even further, when the wall was completed (in just fifty-two days!), Nehemiah did not seek to create dependency on his skills or to create wealth and fame for himself. Indeed, he turned the city's management over to others. If you want to be a great leader, always consider the People around you as well as the Task. And when possible, include those who work *with* you, *for* you, and even those *over* you. Everyone will benefit from the process even as they complete the Task! Then it is time for celebration. Completion of the *Task* is recognized, but the *People* get rewarded.

This noble tree is a good representation of Nehemiah, who understood the necessary balance between Tasks and People. It demonstrates extensive Abilities, strong but not overwhelming Authority, and the presumption of substantial Character.

Source of photo unknown

The Three Perspectives of a Leader

After viewing a television program on which I had been interviewed, I was upset by how I looked. "Am I that ugly?" I asked my husband. He was quiet for a moment and then said, "I recognized you." (Reader's Digest, contributed by Jane D. Garrison)

A smile is the best way to get away with trouble even if it's a fake one. (Anonymous)

To be rather than to seem. (State Motto of North Carolina)

In chapter 10 we learned about the differences between the way we see ourselves, the way others see us, and the Real Us. Business etiquette consultant Lydia Ramsey has pointed out that it takes an average of seven seconds for a person to make a judgment about you based on your initial meeting. So she gives some tips on making a powerful first impression:

- Learn what people use to form their first opinion. When you meet someone face-to-face, 93 percent of how you are judged is based on nonverbal data—appearance and body language—while only 7 percent is influenced by the words that you speak.
- Choose your first few words carefully. Even though it may be only 7 percent, those first few words can be vital. Words of appreciation are a good choice.
- Use the other person's name immediately. People love the sound of their name!
- Match your body language to your verbal message. Smile. Make eye contact. Lean in toward the other person. Show that you are interested and interesting!

I would emphasize the importance of doing your best to make those first impressions *genuine.* You *can* be yourself and put your best foot forward at the same time.

Trees don't pretend. They are what they are. Yet our perceptions of trees can vary with our own perspectives or circumstances.

Girls are like apples on trees. The best ones are at the top of the tree. The boys don't want to reach for the good ones because they are afraid of falling and getting hurt. Instead, they just get the rotten apples from the ground that aren't as good, but easy. So the apples at the top think something is wrong with them, when in reality, they're amazing. They just have to wait for the right boy to come along, the one who's brave enough to climb all the way to the top of the tree.

"Get real." How often have you heard that statement? I heard a sermon once on the topic of being real, through and through. The minister told of buying what was advertised as a red wood picnic table. He expected it to be made of California redwood, which is a strong, long-lasting type of wood. But when he began to assemble the table, he found that it was just white pine with a red stain. A piece broke off in his hand. When he called the store to complain, they said it was a wood table, and it was red. That's all the advertisement said.

Leaders can be like that table. What they claim to be or appear to be on the surface is not always what they are like inside or what is really in their hearts. Leaders can present or promote themselves in ways that get attention, make great initial impressions, and generally mislead others. But sooner or later appearances are replaced with reality.

It is so much better to be "real" from the start. People appreciate genuineness in leaders. A real—authentic—leader doesn't have to maintain an act, or remember what it takes to make the impression he or she wants. Real leaders make real impressions.

Trees, of course, don't have eyes or even a consciousness (as far as we can tell). But if they did, I'm pretty sure they might look something like this:

From Internet

Leaders have subconscious images of themselves that reflect what is important to them, influenced by their values, goals, and dreams. Rarely do we get a good look at that internal image. Some leaders try, at least, to be open about who they think they are, while others will hide at any cost what they know or believe to be true about themselves. The most effective Tree-Dimensional Leaders will be honest with themselves about their self-image. They will seek and accept leadership roles that are compatible with who they are.

Let's take a look at some various "Tree-spectives":

This unusual view of a "retired" root system reminds us of the importance of Character and the lasting impact it can have.

Photo by Author

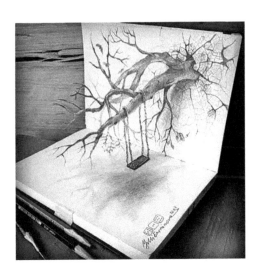

This view of branches (Abilities) is certainly not typical, but does demonstrate a different perspective!

Earthporm.com

What type of tree do you think this is? It seems to have a strong trunk (Authority) and well-developed branch system (Abilities).

Photo by Adriana Franco, pandotrip.com

Only problem is, it's a view from space! That would have to be a pretty large tree, right? Well, no, it is a satellite image of a river system!

Now what have we here? You probably figured pretty quickly that these are close-up views of various types of tree bark—the faces of Authority, so to speak.

From Allen Paterson, <u>Best Trees for Your Garden: photographs by Steven Wooster</u>

Here's a look at a perspective emphasizing Authority:

Photograph by Author

Now one more illustration just to really throw you off. While it has nothing to do with trees or Leadership, it is a great illustration of the impact of Perspective:

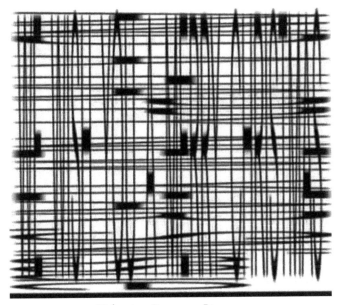

Valentina Pezza on Pinterest

Tilt the page forward, so that you are viewing the illustration from the bottom edge of the page, with the page almost flat. Now turn the page to the left and do the same thing. Wow, huh?

Reading the Rings

When you study the image of a tree as representing Leadership, consider the functions of *primary* and *secondary* features: Let the main, or primary, branches represent primary Abilities—those that are the strongest, most noticeable, most important. Secondary (and tertiary, etc.) branches can represent less vital Abilities. The same can be said for Character traits—the tap root, if you will, supplemented by other roots that branch out from the primary one. As with actual trees, there are fewer options for Authority traits—the trunk— but indeed trees can have primary and secondary trunks, just as leaders can make use of primary and secondary Authority.

12

Presidents, Pundits and Pooh Bahs

jkinako4.wordpress.com

Then he told this parable: *"A man had a fig tree planted in his vineyard; and he came looking for fruit on it and found none. So he said to the gardener, 'See here! For three years I have come looking for fruit on this fig tree, and still I find none. Cut it down! Why should it be wasting the soil?' He replied, 'Sir, let it alone for one more year, until I dig around it and put manure on it. If it bears fruit next year, well and good; but if not, you can cut it down.'"*
—Luke 13:6–9, NRSV

L eaders, like trees, are planted, nourished, and expected to produce. When they don't produce, they may be subject to the
saw. Manure indeed, may be a great cure for what ails leadership in
today's world! In this final chapter, we will contemplate the grand
forest of famous, not-so-famous, and sometimes foolish leaders
whose silhouettes have defined the landscapes of the past, present,
and future. We will wander through the jungle of juggernauts who
have laid claim to leadership. In other words, we will ponder the
profiles of some Presidents, Pundits, and Poo Bahs. (Sorry—sometimes I find alliteration to be irresistible.)

*I recognize my limits
but when I look around
I realize I am not living
exactly in a world of giants.
(Giulio Andreotti)*

*I would rather be
right than President.
(Henry Clay)*

President: *An officer appointed or elected to preside over an organized body of persons. A person who presides. (Dictionary.com)*

Pundit: *A person who pontificates opinions whether you ask for
them or not, and who believes such opinions are necessary, correct, and
irrefutable. In election cycles, pundits can tell you everything there is to
know about what presidential candidates should say and do in order
to be elected. (This, of course, is my own definition, which is not really
accurate, but it IS my opinion ...)*

Pooh Bah: *A pompous, self-important person (Dictionary.com).
Pooh Bahs think they should be presidents (me).*

What makes a great president? Author Doris Kearns Goodwin
addressed this question in *Parade* magazine (Sept. 14, 2008). In her
view, we should use the leadership styles of successful past presidents

as a yardstick when considering current candidates. We have rich resources in the historical records of such presidents as Lincoln and Franklin Roosevelt. She identified ten attributes to look for:

1. **The courage to stay strong.** *(I would place this in the Character/Roots dimension.)* Goodwin notes that Franklin Roosevelt emerged from his ordeal of polio with "greater powers of concentration and greater self-knowledge."

2. **Self-confidence.** *(This is my Authority/Trunk dimension.)* Goodwin explains that Abraham Lincoln demonstrated this trait when he appointed his three chief rivals for the Republican nomination to Cabinet positions and filled other top jobs with former Democrats.

3. **An ability to learn from errors.** *(Obvious Ability/Branches dimension.)* When New Deal programs weren't working, FDR replaced them with new ones.

4. **A willingness to change.** *(Ability/Branches dimension.)* History is replete with examples of presidents successfully changing policies or tactics as needs dictated.

5. **Emotional intelligence.** *(Character/Roots dimension.)* In chapter 3 (*"What is Leadership?"*) I touched on this element of leadership, made popular by Daniel Goleman. The editors of *U. S. News & World Report* (January 14, 2002) defined it as "the capacity to handle your own emotions and your relationships with others." They ask "Is it 'brains'— knowledge, logic, and rational thought? Or is it this alternative kind of intelligence based on feelings? Or is it a combination of the two that counts most?" The USN&WR editors point out that any good leader will have a "healthy dose" of both rational thought and emotional intelligence. They recalled the 2000 election campaign between George W. Bush and Al Gore, in which pundits (don't you just love that word?) said Bush lacked knowledge, and Gore lacked emotion; it was the scarecrow vs. the tin man—EQ versus IQ. And the election ended in a near-tie.

6. **Self-control.** *(My Ability/Branches dimension.)* Lincoln was famous for writing "hot letters" when he was angry at someone, and then setting the letters aside until he calmed down, never mailing them. Roosevelt exhibited uncanny calm after the attack on Pearl Harbor, as did John Kennedy during the Cuban missile crisis.

7. **A popular touch.** *(Character/Roots.)* More accurately, Goodwin apparently intended this characteristic to mean "in touch with the public." She cites examples of Lincoln and Roosevelt having special awareness of public sentiment, and a sense of timing for implementing a policy or action.

8. **A moral compass.** *(Character/Roots.)* This could indeed be the single most important characteristic of any Leader. What greater calling can one have than to lead with a moral compass? The greatest presidents secured their places in history by holding firm to what they believed to be right (freedom for slaves, supporting England in early WWII, etc.).

9. **A capacity to relax.** *(Character/Roots and/or Ability/Branches.)* FDR held a cocktail hour every evening just for fun conversation. Lincoln was known for his sense of humor and his ability to "whistle off sadness."

10. **A gift for inspiring others.** *(Character/Roots.)* Alongside having a moral compass, this gift is what makes great leaders great. Memorable presidents were able to use a profound sense of history, poetry and drama to tell stories and use metaphors to move the American public.

I have consistently maintained that any list of leadership characteristics can be organized into the categories of **Authority, Abilities, and Character.** Goodwin's list of leadership styles of successful past presidents provides an excellent opportunity to demonstrate this concept. Here is that list in a *Tree-Dimensional* view:

Abilities:

An ability to learn from errors.
A willingness to change.
A capacity to relax.

Authority:

Self-confidence.
Self-control.

Character:

The courage to stay strong.
Emotional intelligence.
A popular touch.
A moral compass.
A gift for inspiring others.

Background: Crows-Feathers-Art

In his study of the presidency, *Hail to the Chief*, historian Robert Dallek lists five qualities that have been constants in the men who have most effectively fulfilled the oath of office (my words in italics): (1) **vision** (*Authority* and *Character*); (2) **political pragmatism** (*Ability*); (3) **national consensus** (*Ability*); (4) **personal connection with the people** (*Character*); and (5) **credibility** (*Character*). Dallek places the greatest emphasis on numbers 4 and 5. "The force of presidential personality has been a major factor in determining a president's fate …

[P]residents who are unable to earn the trust of their countrymen are governors who cannot govern and lead" (as quoted in *The Amateur*, p. 83).

So here is the *Tree-Dimensional version*:

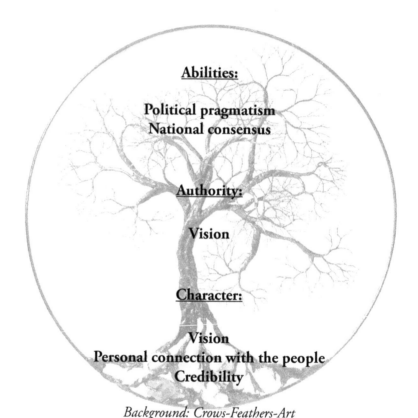

Abilities:

Political pragmatism
National consensus

Authority:

Vision

Character:

Vision
Personal connection with the people
Credibility

Background: Crows-Feathers-Art

Edward Klein (in *The Amateur*, p. 228) refers to the adage that nothing prepares a person to be president: "It certainly wasn't true of George Washington, Abraham Lincoln, Franklin Roosevelt, Dwight Eisenhower, and Ronald Reagan. All of them were eminently suited for the presidency, because they had the temperament (*Authority*), management skills (*Abilities*), and vision (*Character*) to tackle the job."

In 2004, *Reader's Digest* conducted an online poll about qualities we look for in a president. The rankings below reflect the percentage of people who said the attribute was extremely or very important:

Qualities We Look for in a President

Say what they mean, mean what they say	93%
Never shades the truth	85
Good delegator	71
Someone you admire	71
Held consistent views throughout career	71
Demonstrates genuine humility	70
Genuinely intellectual	63
Seeks Presidency out of a sense of duty	63
Unfailingly loyal to staff	54
Always speaks diplomatically	47
Reaches decisions by consensus	47
An activist who promises real change	46
Charismatic speaker	42
Relies heavily on an inner circle of advisors	31
Served in the military	30
Comes across like the "guy next door"	30
A politician well liked by fellow politicians	29
Has traveled the world extensively	22
An outsider to Washington, DC	13
Independently wealthy	5

Things have probably changed quite a lot since 2004, and certainly your own opinions may vary wildly from these. But people *do* have their opinions (pundits let us know that), and this also demonstrates why we have the two-party system in which supporters take amazingly diverse stands on seemingly simple choices. Certainly the two lowest-rated qualities above don't jibe with the popularity of Donald J. Trump in the 2016 campaign!

As democracy is perfected, the office of the President represents, more and more closely, the inner soul of the people. On some great and glorious day, the plain folks of the land will reach their heart's desire at last and the White House will be occupied by a downright fool and complete narcissistic moron.
(H. L. Mencken, July 26, 1920)

So now, let's take the *Reader's Digest* list of desired presidential qualities and convert them to the *Tree-Dimensional* categories.

Abilities:

Good delegator
Genuinely intellectual
Always speaks diplomatically
Served in the military
Has traveled the world extensively
An outsider to Washington, DC
Independently wealthy

Authority:

Say what they mean, mean what they say
Held consistent views throughout career
Reaches decisions by consensus
An activist who promises real change
Relies heavily on an inner circle of advisors

Character:

Never shades the truth
Someone you admire
Demonstrates genuine humility
Seeks Presidency out of a sense of duty
Unfailingly loyal to staff
Charismatic speaker
Comes across like the "guy next door"
A politician well liked by fellow politicians

Background: Crows-Feathers-Art

Notice that there are more Character (Roots) and Abilities (Branches) traits than Authority (Trunk) traits. Just as it should be!

Presidential scholar and author Richard Reeves, in the article explaining this poll, points out that what we want in a president is not always what makes for a successful presidency. Still, American voters bring their opinions to the voting booth every four years. Reeves presents examples of situations where presidents violated many of these poll preferences, usually for good reasons that benefitted the country. Great presidents have lied, misdirected the American people, been inconsistent, and have rarely been humble. Reeves notes that "it makes more sense to acknowledge the toughness of this job of President, and the need to be shrewd and manipulative to do it well." He believes that judgment is perhaps the most important quality needed in an effective president. History usually judges presidents by how they handle one or two big, often unexpected situations.

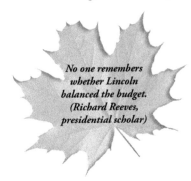

No one remembers whether Lincoln balanced the budget. (Richard Reeves, presidential scholar)

Abraham Lincoln

Photo by Michael Nichols

Abraham Lincoln was arguably the most well-known and well-respected of all US presidents. He towers above others as a giant in the world of politics and leaders in general. Yet as time progresses, even such icons as Lincoln gain their critics, and history seems to dredge up information that makes them more human than godlike.

We might all agree, however, that Lincoln exhibited an incomparable image of Authority (thus the humongous trunk in the above image). His Abilities (branches), while used effectively when needed, were not really extensive. He was a talented public speaker, wrote with precision and persuasion, and could wrestle and chop wood with the best of them. But there are other presidents who had much more extensive arsenals of talents and skills. The root system of my "Lincoln Tree" above *must* be one helluva sight! In the same way, Lincoln's Character—in the broad sense of the word as I define it—was simply incomparable. That, above all, is what distinguishes Honest Abe from all other presidents, and indeed from most other leaders in any category.

Nearly all men can stand adversity, but if you want to test a man's character, give him power.
(Abraham Lincoln)

If I had eight hours to chop down a tree, I'd spend six hours sharpening my ax.
(Abraham Lincoln)

According to Eliot A. Cohen in <u>Supreme Command: Soldiers, Statesmen and Leadership in Wartime (2002)</u>, President Lincoln's qualifications to serve as commander-in-chief were infinitely inferior to those of his protagonist, Jefferson Davis. A West Point graduate, Davis had many years of active military experience leading regiments through battle. He served four years as Secretary of War before becoming president of the Confederacy. Lincoln, on the other hand served only a few token months as a junior militia officer in the Black Hawk war of 1832. In that role, he lost a wrestling match with another captain to decide whose company would occupy a choice campground.

Yet Cohen claims, Lincoln was easily the greater war leader. "Davis did not have the reservoirs of humor, patience, and sympathy that allowed his opponent to put up with the misbehavior and failures of military commanders."

Both Lincoln and Davis had earned or been granted the **Authority** they needed to lead. Both had unusual **Abilities** suited to the challenges they faced. At this level of analysis, both Lincoln and Davis were excellent *two-dimensional* leaders with strengths in the areas of **Authority** and **Ability**. But Lincoln's qualities of humor, patience, and sympathy gave him the edge. These qualities can be considered as elements of the "third Dimension" of Leadership that I call **Character**. And that dimension is what made Abraham Lincoln an icon for the ages.

The best way to destroy an enemy is to make him your friend. (Abraham Lincoln)

Sir, my concern is not whether God is on my side; my greatest concern is to be on God's side, for God is always right. (Abraham Lincoln)

When Lincoln appointed the imperfect General Joseph Hooker to his command, he wrote the following letter in 1863. It artfully demonstrates how to cultivate and make use of a subordinate who may be flawed, but who has the will and energy to be useful:

I have placed you at the head of the Army of the Potomac.... And yet I think it best for you to know that there are some things in regard to which I am not quite satisfied with you. I believe you to be a brave and a skillful soldier, which, of course, I like.... You have confidence in yourself, which is a valuable, if not an indispensable, quality. You are ambitious, which, within reasonable bounds, does good rather than harm. I have heard...of your recently saying that both the Army and the government needed a dictator. Of course it was not for this, but in spite of it, that I have given you the command.... I much fear that the spirit which you have aided to infuse into the Army, of criticizing their Commander, and withholding confidence from him, will now turn upon you. I shall assist you as far as I can, to put it down. Neither you, nor Napoleon, if he were alive again, could get any good out of an army, while such a spirit prevails in it.

And now, beware of rashness... but with energy, and sleepless vigilance, go forward, and give us victories.

According to Cohen, this letter "administered both rebuke and encouragement with a paternal air of concern." Lincoln shared with Robert E. Lee the art of making use of able but imperfect subordinates. On the other hand, he was extremely tough on those who failed to perform. Lincoln demonstrated the rare quality of combining humanity with toughness. He has, of course, been criticized for condoning—even encouraging—such ruthlessness as Sherman's devastating march through the South. Some Pundits can't distinguish between flexibility and inconsistency. Great leaders can use the most appropriate leadership tools for the task at hand, even if they may seem inconsistent.

I am not bound to win, but I am bound to be true. I am not bound to succeed, but I am bound to live by the light that I have. I must stand with anybody that stands right, and stand with him while he is right, and part with him when he goes wrong.
(Abraham Lincoln)

My great concern is not whether you have failed, but whether you are content with failure.
(Abraham Lincoln)

Another defining characteristic of Lincoln involves the principle of *Perspective*. He had no illusions. One of Lincoln's secretaries observed that "He had his hopes and desires, but he did not commit the strategic sin that Napoleon described of 'making pictures' of the world as one wishes it to be, rather than as it is."

Reminisce Extra magazine, in a 1993 special edition, tells a heart-wrenching story about a little girl who had lost contact with her Confederate soldier father. She bravely wrote President Lincoln a letter pleading for him to let her father come home. To the family's amazement, the child received the following letter from Mr. Lincoln himself:

My dear little rebel... My heart is burdened with the thought that so many children in the North and South are grieving for their absent fathers. May God care for those who are forced apart. We must pray for peace... and if it is so that your father can return, he shall have safe passage home.

Note that Lincoln did not promise what he could not deliver, but he demonstrated his concern for the child's agony and gave her hope. Sadly, the child and her family discovered later that the father had been wounded and was being cared for by a minister, but ultimately died before he could return home. The mortally wounded soldier had managed to hand carve a gift for his beloved daughter, which was given to her by the minister several years after the war ended!

Summary, Abraham Lincoln:

Abilities
A few truly gifted talents, used magnificently, appropriately, yet modestly.

Authority
Highest level; broad, earned, learned and granted.

Character
Greatest among all Presidents. Integrity, humor, caring, unwavering convictions.

I am a success today because I had a friend who believed in me and I didn't have the heart to let him down.
(Abraham Lincoln)

Barack Obama

Photo by Author

I am not a fan of Barack Obama. No, I will not refund your money for buying my book. Certainly I know that Mr. Obama has legions of fans who remain convinced that he is close to the Messiah. If you are one of those people, you can tear out these pages if you wish. If it hadn't been too expensive, I would have asked the publisher to perforate the Obama pages to facilitate that. I believe the above tree represents Obama quite well, except it doesn't lean enough to the left. (I will give you a minute for that to soak in.) This tree, like Obama, has a very tall, but thin Authority trunk (he did get elected to two terms as president, after all). There is very visible Authority, but it is not innate, natural, nor substantial; he only has Authority because it was granted to him (temporarily, thank goodness) by election. There are very few Ability branches, and they are all bunched at the top. He had a mediocre academic record (as far as we know), sharpened his skills as a community organizer, for heaven's sake, and served one inconsequential term as a senator! What Abilities he does demonstrate, he learned/gained only after he was elected and served as president—thus, bunched at the top. Pine trees are infamous for having shallow root systems (Character), and this quite adequately represents Barack Obama's Character (in my opinion, of course). He has enough Character traits to hold up the trunk and branches, such as a decent sense of humor, is persuasive as a public speaker (as long as there is a teleprompter), and has a mystical charismatic personality that virtually hypnotizes his followers. Otherwise, he is a pine tree.

Photo by Author

Or perhaps a boojum tree:

http://imgc.artprintimages.com

We have never gone wrong when we have expanded rights and responsibilities to include everybody. (Barack Obama, June 15, 2012)

In his best-selling book *The Amateur* (2012), New York Times author Edward Klein quotes a number of people who had close ties to Obama. Most of them were, shall we say, unflattering. One historian who had met with Obama, but prefers to remain anonymous, said, *Obama hasn't been able to capture the public's imagination and inspire people to follow him. Vision isn't enough in a President. Great presidents not only have to enunciate their vision; they must lead by example and inspiration. Franklin Roosevelt spoke to the individual. He and Ronald Reagan had the ability to make each American feel that the president cared deeply and personally about them.... The American people have come to realize that, in Barack Obama, they elected a man as president who does not know how to lead. He lacks an executive sense. He doesn't know how to run things. He's not a manager. He hasn't been able to bring together the best and brightest talents. Not to put too fine a point on it, he's in over his head.*

The future rewards those who press on. I don't have time to feel sorry for myself. I don't have time to complain. I'm going to press on.
(Barack Obama)

If you're walking down the right path and you're willing to keep walking, eventually you'll make progress.
(Barack Obama)

My friends, we live in the greatest nation in the history of the world. I hope you'll join with me as we try to change it.
(Barack Obama)

I think that I am a better speechwriter than my speechwriters. I know more about policies on any particular issue than my policy directors. And I'll tell you right now that I'm gonna think I'm a better political director than my political director.
(Barack Obama)

It's here that companies like Solyndra are leading the way toward a brighter and more prosperous future.
(Barack Obama)

People say I'm arrogant and aloof. Some people are so dumb.
(Barack Obama)

Presidential historian Fred I. Greenstein was quoted in *The Amateur* (p. 79) as saying:

With all of Obama's rhetorical brilliance and flash, he went into the phone booth as Superman and came out as Clark Kent.

Douglas Baird, former Dean who hired Obama to teach at the Chicago Law School, had this to say (p. 22):

Of course I grant you that it's one thing to be a charismatic figure and walk into a room and excite students, and quite another thing to be a leader—to hire people, motivate people, and manage decision-making. That's not something Barack experienced or learned at the Chicago Law School. I know people in the White House, and I don't get a sense from my conversations with them that there's anything in Barack's experience as a law professor that prepared him for the leadership part of the presidential job.

David Sheiner, MD, Barack Obama's personal physician, said on page 17: *he's academic, lacks passion and feeling, and doesn't have the sense of humanity that I expected.*

And finally, this short but sweet observation by Steven Rogers, Gund Family Distinguished Professor of Entrepreneurship at Northwestern University's Kellogg School of Management: *What you have with Barack Obama is a lack of character (p. 33).*

Summary, Barack Obama:

Abilities
Public speaking. Learned some skills in on-the-job training.

Authority
Elected president. Self-confidence. Not much else.

Character
**Shallow. Lack of integrity.
Notable sense of humor. Charismatic,
can inspire many people.**

Dwight D. Eisenhower

Photo by Author

Perhaps because he was the first president I remember while growing up, I have always considered Eisenhower as the epitome of what a president should be. He manifested a gentle grandfatherly image—one of Character, Authority, and Abilities with complete authenticity. We have not had a president with his attributes since.

Rick Atkinson, in the October 28, 2002, issue of *U. S. News & World Report*, described Eisenhower as having *"an incandescent grin ... But the face was far more than a smile. His eyes were wide-set and unwandering, his head broad-browed and perfectly centered over squared shoulders. Both his face and his hands moved perpetually, and he exuded a magnetic amiability that made most men want to please him. Perhaps that was because, as one admirer asserted, they intuited he was 'good and right in the moral sense', or perhaps it was because, as a British air marshal concluded, 'Ike has the qualities of a little boy which make you love him.'"*

Eisenhower's background is reminiscent of that of Abraham Lincoln. He was the third son of a Midwestern failed merchant. He basically stumbled into a military career because West Point provided a free education. Unremarkable as a cadet, he also started out with an undistinguished career as a staff officer, and remained in the rank of major for sixteen years. Atkinson states that *"his worldview seemed conventional, his gifts commensurate with the modesty he exuded. Yet he possessed enough depth to resist easy plumbing ...* (I love that analogy, visualizing a grand tree with an incomprehensible root system.) ... *His sincerity and native fairness were so transparent that they obscured an incisive intellect.... His rapid rise would forever remain something of a mystery, a convergence of talent, opportunity, and fortune so improbable that to many it seemed providential."*

Even as late as December of 1942, after being promoted to the rank of lieutenant general and commander of the North African campaign, he was hardly held in high regard by the Allied military. The foremost British officer at the time, Gen. Alan Brooke, wrote in his diary "Eisenhower as a general is hopeless! He submerges himself in politics and neglects his military duties, partly, I am afraid, because he knows little if anything about military matters.... Deficient of experience and of limited ability."

After a series of poor decisions punctuated with bad luck, Eisenhower learned from his mistakes, made necessary adjustments, and exhibited strength of character and competence. He had developed the "traits of authenticity, vigor, and integrity .... He had displayed admirable grace and character under crushing strain.... The failings of deficient commanders had taught him to be tougher, even ruthless, with subordinates" (see Lincoln above). His son John wrote, "North Africa transformed him ... from a mere person to a personage ... full of authority, and truly in command."

Yet when he was in the White House, Eisenhower had the strength of character and the wisdom to rise above his convictions. On the issue of integration, he privately lobbied Chief Justice Earl Warren to uphold the doctrine of "separate but equal," but publicly yielded to the concept of law for the good of the country and because it was the right thing to do.

Dwight D. Eisenhower served as President for two terms, from 1953–1961. It came as a surprise when my research revealed that he was succeeded by John F. Kennedy! That was a huge transition in American history and culture. Seems as if some more modern president should have been between Eisenhower and Kennedy. I mean Eisenhower was in black and white, and Kennedy was in color, for heaven's sake!

His major accomplishments included keeping pressure on the Soviet Union, balancing the budget, supporting the Republic of China in Taiwan, ending the Korean War, establishing NASA, the Interstate Highway System, the National Defense Education Act, and the Atomic Energy Act. Although it is apparently not widely remembered, President Eisenhower avoided a huge crisis involving use of nuclear weapons against China. During the conflict over US protection of Taiwan in 1954, all of Eisenhower's military and foreign policy experts urged him on at least five occasions, to launch an atomic attack against China. While he openly threatened the Chinese with use of nuclear weapons, he kept them guessing and consistently refused the advice of the experts. In the end, he accomplished his objectives of confronting communism while keeping world peace. Through this accomplishment, Eisenhower demonstrated his unique "dual" Authority derived from both his military and presidential experience. He survived a serious heart attack and a stroke while in office, initiated the concept of Air Force One and ushered into the union the states of Alaska and Hawaii. While he inevitably had critics, as all presidents do, Eisenhower was voted Gallup's most admired man twelve times, achieving widespread popular esteem.

Summary, Dwight D. Eisenhower:

Abilities:
Delegating; learning from mistakes;
seeing the "big picture";
incisive intellect.

Authority:
Notable for both his military and
presidential Authority
(Close inspection of the tree image above
will reveal twin trunks.)
Subordinates wanted to please him.

Character:
Strong personal convictions,
but with a sense of the greater good;
"good and right in the moral sense";
sincerity; fairness.

Ronald Reagan

Photo by Author

The fortieth president of the United States, Ronald Wilson Reagan had diverse and successful careers as a lifeguard, radio sports announcer, military officer, actor, president of the Screen Actors Guild, motivational speaker, two terms as governor of California, and two terms as president. The tree image above is quite suited to Reagan's leadership, portraying the wide variety of his Abilities (branches), Authority (multiple trunks), and Character (presumptively extensive root system).

Michael Barone, in a June 2004 article in US News & World Report, used the occasion of Reagan's funeral to ruminate about his legacy. Barone noted that speakers at the funeral cited biblical references to "a city that is set on a hill" and "a city on a hill," bases for Reagan's belief that America is "a shining city on a hill." President Bush, quoting William F. Buckley, said "Reagan is indisputably a part of America."

Friendliness and openness defined America's character, and Reagan infused them in its politics.
(Michael Barone)

Roger Simon, in the same issue of US News & World Report (June 2004), noted that Reagan was "always keeping track of the goal, never keeping track of the clock." (My oh my, do I love that line. My friends and business associates will attest to that!) Critics worried that Reagan would become seventy within a few weeks of his inauguration. Reagan didn't care. He was eternally optimistic, largely because things had always worked out for him.

Barone compared Reagan to Franklin Roosevelt, pointing out that both came to office when people had given up on the economy, and both brought it back to prosperity and abundance. At those times, the American people had lost confidence in the greatness of their country and its values; there was an air of despondency. Interestingly, Roosevelt and Reagan brought about needed change in vastly different—even opposing—ways: Roosevelt by expanding government and Reagan by cutting. Reagan always admired Roosevelt, even though he opposed many of his policies. There is such a great lesson in leadership here: Success and greatness can often depend on the circumstances; great leaders focus their dimensions of Authority, Abilities, and Character in directions needed at the time. They balance Nature/Nurture, Positive/Negative factors, Task/People strategies, and Perspective to accomplish their goals.

Roosevelt and Reagan, while quite different politically and philosophically, shared Character traits. Both were optimistic, open and friendly; yet each had "cold steel beneath the smiles" and "grace under pressure." Barone notes that Reagan, after he was shot, stood, and walked from the ambulance into the hospital, taking care to button his jacket! And of course, his sense of humor was legendary—from "I won't use the youth and inexperience of my opponent for political purposes" to his joke about a Republican standing on a pile of manure saying it was the first time he had ever given a speech from a Democratic platform.

For Ronald Reagan, the world of legend and myth is a real world. He visits it regularly, and he's a happy man there. (Patrick Buchanan, former White House communications director, 1988)

When Reagan took office, the view of outgoing President Jimmy Carter was that America was in "a malaise." Reagan knew that what America needed was a leader who could inspire confidence and hope, just as he had done in the movies. He saw himself as one of us—as an integral part of the American people, of America itself. He had no doubts about the future of his country, and therefore neither did those who supported him.

And whatever else history may say about me when I'm gone, I hope it will record that I appealed to your best hopes, not your worst fears, to your confidence rather than your doubts. (Ronald Reagan)

I now begin the journey that will lead me into the sunset of my life. I know that for America there will always be a bright dawn ahead. (Ronald Reagan)

There have been times in this office when I've wondered how you could do the job if you hadn't been an actor. (Ronald Reagan)

<u>Summary, Ronald Reagan:</u>

<u>Abilities</u>
Communication, public speaking; diplomacy;
acting; persuasion; "common sense"
intelligence; seeing the "big picture".

<u>Authority</u>
Notable for multiple levels of Authority,
including acting roles, union leadership,
governor, and president. His life was filled
with leadership accomplishments.

<u>Character</u>
Strong personal convictions; sincerity;
likeability; Christian; credibility; charisma;
patriotism; optimism; sense of humor.

George W. Bush

Wikipedia.org/olive trees

George Bush's presidency was, of course, defined—or more accurately, redefined—by the events of 9/11. His legacy would certainly have been quite different if that day had been like any other. Now forever linked to the War on Terror, he would have been remembered more—if those attacks had not happened—for his policies and accomplishments relative to the economy, health care, education, social security reform, immigration reform, tax cuts, No Child Left Behind Act, Partial-Birth Abortion Ban Act, Medicare prescription benefits for seniors, AIDS relief program PEPFAR—and heaven knows what else. But like too many Presidents before him, his life and the lives of all of us were fundamentally changed in a heartbeat when unanticipated world events intervened.

While George Bush was reared and educated in privileged surroundings within a highly political family (thus the grove of trees in the above photo), his childhood and early career did not exactly prepare him for greatness. His academic credentials were unremarkable, by his own accounts; his grade average at Yale was seventy-seven (still, that was at YALE—many of us could not even get *admitted* to Yale). He was the head cheerleader in high school, a cheerleader in college, and drank a lot. Critics claim that his military career was tainted with favoritism, weak pilot aptitude test scores, and irregular attendance, and he was finally suspended from flying.

Bush made some wise (or lucky) investments in the oil business, which then allowed him to buy into the Texas Rangers baseball team, which turned into a $15 million profit. His initial foray into politics was unsuccessful, but he continued to make contacts and chalk up minor accomplishments through his father's presidency. With good timing on his side, he became governor of Texas in 1995 and then built enough of a legacy to vault him into the US presidency in 2001.

Stephen G. Smith, an editor of US News & World Report, spent some time observing Bush during his transition from governor to president (U. S. News & World Report, January 22, 2001). On the first occasion, Smith developed concerns about Bush's leadership, describing him as "more tentative and less magnetic" than portrayed by the press. Bush was shallow on foreign and domestic policy, but he did demonstrate a genuine concern about how people deal with problems in their lives.

I felt he (George W. Bush) came through the screen in an unprepossessing way— uncomfortable before the cameras, hesitant in his answers, smaller than his actual size, lacking the presidential manner of, say, Ronald Reagan and Bill Clinton. (Stephen G. Smith, Editor, USN & WR)

Less than two weeks from Bush's inauguration, however, Mr. Smith again interviewed the then-president-elect. He was struck by the way he had changed, noting that "the campaign had transformed him." Smith likened Bush to a natural athlete who had "trained to a world-class standard." Now he exuded confidence, with forceful body language such as leaning in to his listener when making a point.

The man had become part of an institution greater than himself. George W. Bush sped into the night, every bit a president. (Stephen G. Smith)

One thing that served Bush well was his sense of humor—which I consider vital in a Leader's arsenal—especially presidents, who live daily in the deepest mire of potential depression and challenges to self-esteem. Former Senator Bob Dole published a book on the topic ("Great Presidential Wit" (Scribner 2001). In an interview about the book with Walt Duka (AARP Bulletin, June 2001), Dole said that George W. Bush was "off to a good start" with humor. Dole cited this exchange Bush had with reporters:

"I don't read half of what you write," Bush said.

"We don't listen to half of what you say," one of the reporters retorted.

To which Bush shot back: "That's apparent in the other half (that I do) read."

Dole says that humor in the job is not so difficult at first when you're successful and the winner because everything is rosy and funny. Then in an ironic statement (this was in June 2001, just three months before the events of September 11), Dole said that Bush knows future events may involve "backing into the buzz saw" and "having his mettle severely tested." (Yes, indeed!)

Second only to backbone, every president requires a funny bone. (Former Senator Bob Dole)

I'm going to depart somewhat from the narrative stream for an aside on some of Senator Dole's observations about presidential humor. His "Top Ten White House Wits" are the following: Abraham Lincoln, Ronald Reagan, Franklin D. Roosevelt, Theodore Roosevelt, Coolidge, Kennedy, Truman, Lyndon Johnson, Hoover, and Wilson.

- Dole describes an example when a "pesky office seeker" approached Lincoln with news that the chief of customs had died. When the man had the gall to ask if he could take his place, Lincoln answered "It's fine with me if the undertaker doesn't mind."
- Reagan said one day, with a twinkle in his eye, "How was I to know when I ordered those B-1s they were airplanes? I thought they were vitamins for the troops."
- Reagan's definition of "status quo" is "Latin for the mess we're in."
- President Kennedy, who served in the Navy aboard PT 109, was once asked how he became a wartime hero. He answered, "It was entirely involuntary. They sank my boat."
- Calvin Coolidge was a man of few words, but they were often funny: When asked what he did for exercise, he said, "I get my picture taken."
- LBJ, after being given a draft of a speech quoting Aristotle, felt that the public wouldn't know "who the #&%$ Aristotle is." So in his speech he used the philosopher's words, but used the lead-in "As my dear old daddy used to say to me ..."
- Bill Clinton did not make Dole's top ten, but he did say that Clinton was "blessed with great speaking ability and talented joke writers."

Now back to the discussion on George W. Bush. While he had a slow start toward the presidency, he had the advantage of an extensive political family; he grew into the role, and actually achieved a level of greatness, if for nothing more than pulling the country together in the immediate aftermath of 9/11. In his book *Decision Points* (Crown Publishers 2010), Bush uses concepts that I really like in describing how he views leadership in others—most of which were reflected in his own leadership. Some of those concepts are (*my own comments in italics*):

- "I started each personnel decision by defining the job description and the criteria for the ideal candidate." He interviewed candidates for major appointments face-to-face. "I used my time to gauge character *(yesss!)* and personality. I was looking for integrity, competence, selflessness, and an ability to handle pressure. I always liked people with a sense of humor, a sign of modesty and self-awareness" (p. 66). *Note his emphasis on my dimensions of Authority, Ability, and Character.*
- "I admired Churchill's courage, principle, and sense of humor—all of which I thought were necessary for leadership" (p. 108). *Yesss!*
- "I read a lot of history, and I was struck by how many presidents had endured harsh criticism. The measure of their character *(yesss!)*, and often their success, was how they responded" (p.121).
- "Rarely had a man met his moment in history more naturally than Rudy Giuliani did on September 11. He was defiant *(Ability)* at the right times, sorrowful *(Character)* at the right times, and in command *(Authority)* the entire time" (p.147).
- "One hallmark of Lincoln's leadership was that he established an affectionate bond with rank-and-file soldiers … His empathy taught a powerful lesson and served as a model for other war presidents to follow" (p.368).

> *The nature of the presidency is that sometimes you don't choose which challenges come to your desk. You do decide how to respond.*
> *(George W. Bush)*

George W. Bush's legacy is yet to be determined. Many historians agree that at least he was one of the most consequential, transformative, and noteworthy presidents in American history. None of that necessarily means that he was a great, or even good, president. (Personally, I think he was a great Leader, in *Tree Dimensional* terms.) A 2010 survey of historians, political scientists, and presidential scholars gave him low ratings on handling the economy, communication, ability to compromise, foreign policy accomplishments, and intelligence.

The tree image I chose to represent Bush is set in a grove of very similar trees, representing the Bush family heritage that strongly influenced George W. The trunk, while not towering over other trees, does represent strong Authority, evidenced by roles as governor of Texas, president, and the respect he had from the military as commander-in-chief. The trunk is gnarled, which is representative of the horrendous strain he faced dealing with terrorism. The branches, while plentiful, are rather bunched at the top because his Abilities became most apparent late in his career after election as president. And the root system (Character) is substantial because I think Bush has deep Character traits.

Summary, George W. Bush:

Abilities
Calm under pressure; sensing value of others; delegating; decision-making; communicating empathy and sincerity; "common sense" intelligence.

Authority
Strong, bolstered by adversity; respect of military; served as governor and president; natural aura of Authority.

Character
Strong personal convictions; sincerity; likeability; Christian; credibility; moderate charisma; patriotism; optimism; sense of humor.

The Worst (?) Presidents

As presidents recede into history, their legacies become less and less flexible and eventually take shape as images that define them. History has not been kind to some.

Wikipedia: Rzuwig   *Photo by author*   *source of photo unknown*

Death Begets Life, Ireena Worthy/Flickr   *Photo by author*   *Photo by author*

U.S. News & World Report (February 26, 2007) ran a special report on "The 10 Worst Presidents" (pp. 40–53). The magazine calculated the average of five major and relatively recent presidential polls and came up with rankings for the ten "least successful presidencies." The following profiles are the top <u>five</u> "worst" from the USN&WR listing. The information is primarily from the USN&WR article, supplemented by other sources:

1. James Buchanan(1857–1861)

James Buchanan/Wikipedia

James Buchanan believed his constitutional duty restrained him from dealing with the looming issues of slavery and threats of secessionism. While he personally rejected slavery as an indefensible evil, he supported weak compromises that permitted the spread of slavery, including the Supreme Court's *Dread Scott* decision which ruled that Congress had no power to limit slavery in the territories.

He was a decent man of Character and faith, with a level of intelligence that should have served him well in the presidency. Yet his unwillingness to exercise Authority, use his Abilities, or follow his conscience (Character) to lead the country resulted in a failed presidency.

To his dying day, he (Buchanan) felt that history would treat him favorably for having performed his constitutional duty. He was wrong. (Jay Tolson, USN&WR, p.44, Feb. 26, 2007)

Just for fun, find Buchanan's tree in the illustrations above.

2. Warren G. Harding(1921–1923)

I am not fit for this office and should never have been here. (Warren G. Harding)

Warren Harding (Harris & Ewing/Public Domain)

Warren G. Harding is rated by many sources as America's worst president. According to *Wikipedia*, "He died one of the most popular presidents in history, but the subsequent exposure of scandals that took place under him, such as Teapot Dome," and revelations of an affair by one of his mistresses *(imagine that!)* eroded his reputation. He was a handsome, affable womanizer. His father once told him it was good that he wasn't born a girl, "because you'd be in the family way all the time. You can't say no." *(Hmmm. Remind you of other former presidents?)*

In 1920, Harding's chances of receiving the Republican nomination were considered nil, but the convention deadlocked over the leading candidates, and Harding gradually gained ground until he was nominated on the tenth ballot! Even then, he did little campaigning, remaining for the most part in his adopted home town of Marion, Ohio, counting on potential supporters to come to him. Yet he won in a landslide over the Democrat and Socialist Party candidates.

Harding appointed some well-regarded figures to his cabinet, and they engineered a major foreign policy achievement regarding limitations to the world's major naval powers. On the other hand, corruption among other cabinet members and extramarital affairs came to light, but did not fully emerge until after his untimely death from a cerebral hemorrhage resulting from heart disease after only two years in office (August 1923).

History has not been kind to Harding; after his death and in the wake of the emerging scandals, a number of writers attacked him unmercifully. Much of what they wrote has been discredited in recent years, and some have pleaded the case that Harding was a much more effective president than his reputation allows. Notre Dame political scientist Peri Arnold says Harding did pick some good advisors, but that he lacked "unusual intellect, notable talents, or much education. His one great talent was an ability to give high-sounding but empty speeches" (U. S. News & World Report, January 26, 2004, p. 55). *(Imagine that!)*

So find a tree in the collection on page 189 that fits Harding.

3. Andrew Johnson(1865–1869)

Andrew Johnson, Matthew Brady, Wikipedia

A tailor by trade, Andrew Johnson was a native North Carolinian who eventually settled in Tennessee, and was elected to the US Senate. He was a staunch supporter of the Union and was the only southerner to retain his seat in the Senate after secession. Lincoln selected him as his running mate in 1864; Johnson became president only a month after becoming vice president. In the ensuing unrest and battles of Reconstruction, Johnson's political ineptitude became glaringly apparent, especially because of an astonishing indifference to the plight of newly-freed African-Americans. He was the first president to be impeached by the House of Representatives, and escaped conviction in the Senate by only one vote.

Andrew Johnson's legacy will forever be tainted by the enormously difficult times that he inherited as president. Still, his personal characteristics are what we ultimately use as a measure of his leadership:

As a tailor, he cut an impressive figure, always immaculately dressed. In addition, he had a powerful personality, which would initially gain interest from supporters. To his disadvantage, however, Johnson was inflexible and not very nimble politically; he was stubborn, had a bristling personality, an enormous sense of self-importance, and was short-sighted.

Historian James Ford Rhodes wrote:

"Johnson acted in accordance with his nature. He had intellectual force but it worked in a groove. Obstinate rather than firm it undoubtedly seemed to him that following counsel and making concessions were a display of weakness ... His pride of opinion, his desire to beat, blinded him to the real welfare of the South and of the whole country."

Johnson is a particular favorite for the bottom of the pile because of his impeachment ... his complete mishandling of Reconstruction policy ... his bristling personality, and his enormous sense of self-importance.
(Glenn W. Lafantasie, Historian)

In 2002, historian Albert Castel took a stern view of Johnson's presidency, saying Johnson "suffered from serious defects of mind and character." According to Castel, Johnson "lacked flexibility and adroitness" and made hasty decisions without foresight.

Finally, and perhaps most importantly, since Johnson was not elected president, he lacked political and moral authority over Congress. Although Johnson had gained the highest office, Castel notes that "he proved incapable of using it in an effective and beneficial manner."

Using what you know of Tree-Dimensional Leadership, find Andrew Johnson's tree-likeness on page 189.

4. Franklin Pierce(1853–1857)

Franklin Pierce, Matthew Brady, Wikipedia

I think that Franklin Pierce got a bum rap. He is generally ranked as the fourth worst president, but for the life of me, I can't quite figure out why. Maybe he was a bad president, but not such a bad leader, and certainly not a failure or a bad person. He was said to be popular and outgoing. A successful lawyer, he was known for his gracious personality, eloquence, and excellent memory (he delivered his inaugural address from memory). He often defended the poor in court at no charge, was honest and tenacious. Perhaps a hint at qualities that don't serve presidents well was the fact that he preferred order, moderation, compromise, and unity.

He even had some excellent military experience, achieving the rank of brigadier general. Perhaps his presidential problems began because of some unfortunate injuries and illness that caused some to believe he exhibited cowardice, when in fact he was quite brave. Ulysses S. Grant wrote after Pierce's death

"Whatever General Pierce's qualifications may have been for the Presidency, he was a gentleman and a man of courage. I was not a supporter of him politically, but I knew him more intimately than I did any other of the volunteer generals" (Wikipedia).

His family life was rather grim, which certainly had an effect on his presidency. His wife, Jane, suffered all of her life with illness and depression. All their children died young. His last son was killed in a tragic train accident as the family was traveling for the inauguration. Pierce and his wife both found their eleven-year-old son's nearly decapitated body crushed under the train car. Pierce did drink heavily throughout his life, and he eventually died from cirrhosis of the liver at age sixty-five. *(I didn't, however, find any notable evidence that his drinking ever caused embarrassment or hindered his performance as president.)*

Pierce was responsible for several noteworthy accomplishments during his presidency. Congress, however, blocked his effort to obtain Cuba from Spain. *(Imagine our world today if that effort had succeeded!)*

It took some deeper research to find the qualities that contributed to Pierce's reputation as having a failed presidency:

- His nomination for the presidency was essentially accidental. He lacked adequate training and temperamental fitness for the position. He was inexperienced and simply not ready for the role of president and was especially ill-prepared for the extreme challenges of the times.
- Probably because of his preference for moderation and compromise, he allowed a divided Congress to take the initiative, especially in matters that eventually led to the Civil War.
- He was credited with ushering in the decline of the Democratic Party, which lasted for nearly seventy years.
- He had difficulty making up his mind, and often reversed his position before finally making a decision.
- His decision-making style gave the general impression of instability.
- He tried to please everyone, and often failed to do so, thereby making many enemies.
- He primarily served as a moderator, not a true leader.
- Perhaps most importantly, Pierce failed to "catch the popular imagination." I think this concept means that he could not entirely grasp what was important to the public, and they sensed it.

By now you should know enough about Tree-Dimensional Leadership to discern for yourself where Franklin Pierce's Leadership Dimensions failed him. Think on it, and then find an appropriate tree for him on page 189.

If you look for the bad in people expecting to find it, you surely will. (Abraham Lincoln)

5. Richard Nixon(1969–1974)

Biography.com

Watergate. Too often, one word can define a person's legacy. Certainly, Richard Nixon and his supporters would have preferred never to have heard this one. Nixon had significant political gifts (Authority and Abilities) and vision (Character), but he also had flawed judgment (Character) and was quite paranoid (a negative Character trait). He was the only president to resign.

Nixon had an outstanding and fast-rising career prior to his fall from grace. According to WhiteHouse.gov/White House Historical Association, Richard Nixon was born in California in 1913 and had a "brilliant record" at Whittier College and Duke University Law School. He became a successful attorney and served as a Navy lieutenant in the Pacific theatre during World War II. When he left the service, he was elected as a congressman from California, and in 1950 was elected to the US Senate. At age thirty-nine, he was tapped as Dwight D. Eisenhower's running mate in 1950.

After serving as Eisenhower's vice president from 1953–1961, Nixon lost the presidential election to John Kennedy in 1960 and ran unsuccessfully for governor of California in 1962. So it was a notable comeback when he defeated Hubert Humphrey to become president in 1969. Before Watergate, Nixon accomplished much as the thirty-seventh US president:

- He ended American involvement in the Vietnam War
- Brought POW's home
- Ended the draft
- Supported new anticrime laws
- Helped create a broad environmental program
- Appointed conservative judges to the Supreme Court
- Improved relations with the USSR
- Opened diplomatic relations with China
- Was president when astronauts made the first moon landing

And then some guys broke into the Democratic National Headquarters to help him get reelected … and neither Nixon's Authority, Abilities, nor especially his Character could withstand the ensuing storm.

For in the multitude of dreams and many words there is also vanity.
(Ecclesiastes 5:7)

President, Pundit, or Poo Bah?

Ibtimes.co.uk

Well, at the time of this writing, Donald J. Trump is indeed the forty-fifth president of the United States. While many may wish that he wasn't, and some even deny it, he is the president. But could he still qualify as a Pundit or a Poo Bah? Mr. Trump is undeniably the most controversial president in our history. You might say there are at least four categories of opinion on the Pundit/Poo Bah question:

1. Those who believe he is the right man at the right time, armed with the perfect(albeit unusual) attributes to Drain the Swamp and Make America Great Again.
2. Those who out of necessity align with his party, but are dismayed and embarrassed at much of what he says and does.
3. Those who accept reality, but oppose his actions and positions at every turn.
4. Those who refuse to accept reality, and will do ANYTHING to interfere with, deny, oppose, or derail his presidency.

But what about *Leadership?* What kind of leader is Donald J. Trump? In the interests of full disclosure, I, dear reader, am in category 1 above. In fact, I am a HUUGE Trump supporter. That being said, I will offer you an analysis of his Tree-Dimensional Leadership profile that is honest and realistic. In an effort to be somewhat objective, let's use the *Reader's Digest* list of desired presidential qualities that I arranged into the categories of Abilities, Authority, and Character (see page 164). I will rate Mr. Trump on a scale of 1–5 for each quality, 5 being the highest rating. Of course, you may disagree with my analysis, but at least the qualities themselves are pretty objective.

Abilities

Good delegator: 4

Surely you would agree that Mr. Trump would never have achieved his levels of success in the business world without delegating duties and responsibilities judiciously. As president, he has bypassed delegation of matters at unprecedented levels *for a president.* But remember that many people voted for him with the expectation that he would depart from traditional politics and run the government more like a business.

Genuinely intellectual: 3

His knee-jerk and emotional actions, responses, and Tweets could dictate an even lower rating here, but I just can't shake the feeling that Trump is smarter than most people think. He knows what he is doing and makes some brilliant moves. He just isn't smart (or humble or patient) enough to let his actions speak for themselves. And I don't think he *wants* the image of an intellectual.

Always speaks diplomatically: 2

Okay, honesty. This would be a **1**, except that at times, on the international stage, Trump has been as diplomatic as any president has ever been. Admittedly, he marches to his own drummer here.

Served in the military: 1

Facts are facts. He did graduate from a military academy although he never served in the armed forces. Still, no president has supported the military as strongly as Donald J. Trump.

Has traveled the world extensively: 4

Trump's business interests have spanned the globe. In addition to actually traveling to foreign countries, he has had extensive dealings and communications with foreign interests. (No, not the Russians!)

An outsider to Washington, DC: 5

I would assign a **10** rating here, but I have to follow the rules.

Independently wealthy: 5

Again, a **10** would work here.

Authority

Say what they mean, mean what they say: 3

His children have maintained that Mr. Trump has never been vague about what he means. Detractors say that President Trump contradicts himself and intimidates people. Supporters point out that very often he is proven right long after the media has made him appear wrong. He certainly has demonstrated strong convictions. So I am taking a vague stance with a **3** rating. Or maybe a **2**. No, a **4**. No, I'll just stick with a **3**.

Held consistent views throughout career: 3

I would really like to give him a higher rating, but if you look at just his political affiliations, he has changed positions and views over time: Democrat prior to 1987; Republican 1987; Reform Party 1999; Democrat 2001–2008; Republican 2009.

PRESIDENTS, PUNDITS AND POOH BAHS

Reaches decisions by consensus: 3

Okay, Trump makes many decisions on his own, but probably has conferred on more decisions than the public knows about. Dealing requires consensus.

An activist who promises real change: 5

Who could deny a **5** rating here? How do you spell D-R-A-I-N T-H-E S-W-A-M-P?

Relies heavily on an inner circle of advisors: 4

He at least relies heavily on family. And again, I think he has some advisors of which the public is not fully aware. (No, not the Russians!)

Character

Never shades the truth: 2

Okay, I agree with many that the *absolute* truth may sometimes be taking a break in Trump's world. But I truthfully ☺ believe that many of Trump's statements are intended as jokes that are not obvious to some; that sometimes he exaggerates; and that sometimes he *insinuates* without actually lying. So, yes, all that may be *shading* the truth. (I'm not condoning it; just stating the facts, ma'am.)

Someone you admire: 4

Now here is where the great divide comes in. Those who admire Trump really admire him; and those who don't really don't. A Gallop poll from 1988 has largely been forgotten, in which Donald Trump was the tenth most admired person in America. So there.

Demonstrates genuine humility: 1

Yes, a zero would be appropriate here.

Seeks presidency out of a sense of duty: 5

Come on now. Donald Trump is one of the world's richest people. He had all the power and influence anyone could want. He could go places without a lot of hullabaloo, and could have all the privacy he wanted. Yet he chose to run for president, knowingly giving up much of that. Duty.

Unfailingly loyal to staff: 3

Honestly, I just don't know yet. In the business world, he was quite loyal to many, but fired those he felt needed replacing.

Charismatic speaker: 5

Look at the unbelievable crowds he drew at every campaign event, and even now at public appearances. And media coverage? Trump received more free media attention than any candidate in history. Just ask Hillary.

Comes across like "the guy next door": 4

Before you go all "what are you thinking?" on me, hear me out. Despite Trump's billionaire status and living in the social stratosphere, he won the election because he got the votes of solid middle/low middle class workers. Coal miners. Auto workers. Truck drivers. Hell, even bikers! These and other good ol' guys and girls saw something in Donald Trump that may seem odd, but it can't be denied. They elected him president.

A politician well-liked by fellow politicians: 1

Well, no.

- So the total score for President Trump adds up to **67** out of a possible **100(67%)**.
- For the Abilities category, his score is **24** of a maximum **35(69%)**.
- For Authority, he garnered **18** of **25(72%)**.
- And he gets **25** of **40 (63%)** for the Character dimension.
- His Authority dimension rates slightly higher than Abilities, and somewhat more than Character.

I haven't done this rating scale for any other president, but my guess is this is pretty accurate, and I believe Trump's ratings would compare rather favorably with any of the great and/or successful presidents! Of course, you are free to disagree.

Donald J. Trump

Credit: from Internet

Pundits and Poo Bahs

I wasn't quite fair to Pundits in the definitions at the beginning of this chapter. I was using my own personal impressions rather than the "real" definition. (You might say I was being a Pundit …) So here is the real deal from Dictionary.com:

Pundit: *1. A learned person, or authority. 2. A person who makes comments or judgments, especially in an authoritative manner; critic or commentator.*

The problem isn't the lack of potential leaders … but a wrongheaded notion of what exactly a leader is. (Bill George, Truly Authentic Leadership, USN & WR, Oct. 30, 2006)

Pay attention to your enemies, for they are the first to discover your mistakes. (Antisthenes)

One needs occasionally to stand aside from the hum and rush of human interests and passions to hear the voices of God. (Anna Julia Cooper)

I'm afraid that most political Pundits these days are solely defined by part 2 of this definition, which doesn't state, impose, or require any *qualifications* for being a Pundit. So practically anyone with an opinion finds an audience, pontificates proudly and is suddenly seen as wise, and something of a leader to be followed. It helps their case if such a person is a movie star or television personality. This is so stupid and over the top that I am not even going to give any examples. You know who they are. *(David Letterman, Stephen Colbert, Seth Meyers, Madonna, Ashley Judd, Kathy Griffin …).* I'm sorry. Their names just leaked out like diarrhea.

Some semi-legitimate Pundits who seem to have gained substantial followings are such commentators as **Chuck Todd, Don Lemon, Dan Rather, and Karl Rove**. Of course there are scores more who are hosts or regular guests on network and cable television. These folks all had backgrounds or professional preparation that could have provided some credibility. The problem with such personalities as Todd,

Lemon, and Rather is that they unabashedly misrepresent themselves as newsmen (and there are such "newswomen" also). Yet they make absolutely no pretense of being objective when covering the actual news. They cannot get more than one sentence of facts out before they feel compelled to "explain" the far-left liberal interpretation, which is also consistently negative and often downright mean. Even if their positions weren't so diametrically opposed to my own, their tone and clear disregard for facts should be obvious to any discerning viewer.

I included **Karl Rove** in this category because he is a very legitimate Pundit, even though I do not always agree with his analyses. At least he has some real qualifications for having opinions on such matters as politics and presidential administrative actions. He has served as a political consultant, policy advisor, and deputy chief of staff for George W. Bush among other things. An argument can be made that Karl Rove is indeed a Tree-Dimensional Leader. Chuck Todd? Don Lemon? Dan Rather? *Covfefe.*

Poo Bahs, on the other hand, go beyond the pundit level by adding the pretense—or inflated sense—of great power, influence, and leadership in general—i.e., Nancy Pelosi, Maxine Waters; Elizabeth Warren, Chuck Schumer, John McCain, and many others.

My most unfavorite Poo Bah of all time is **Nancy Pelosi**. I will go easy on her and only offer my opinion that she is a joke; an embarrassment to the Democratic Party; dense ("You have to pass it before you can read it"); pigheaded; and in a perpetual fog. She ascended to the unbelievable position of Speaker of the US House of Representatives through a series of family connections, lucky moves and gullible constituents. Authority? No. Abilities? Certainly not. Character? *Whaaat?*

Nancy Pelosi *Conservative101.com*   *Photo by Author*

A very close second for unfavorite Poo Bah status is **Maxine Waters**. I mean, c'mon! Admittedly, the lady has had some notable

accomplishments, but they pale beside her spectacular missteps, strange positions, and downright un-American views: i.e., apologizing to Fidel Castro and praising him for providing help to those

Static6.businessinsider.com

who needed to "flee political persecution" and explaining that looters during Los Angeles riots were "mothers who took this opportunity to take some milk." A Tree-Dimensional Leader with well-balanced Authority, Abilities, and Character? Not a chance!

Photo by Author

Elizabeth Warren, *a.k.a.* Pocahontas—Poo Bah extraordinaire. She really could amount to something, if she would just calm down, make sense, and live in the real world. Senator Warren does have some Tree-Dimensional characteristics, but they are misused, and in some cases used too extremely. You might say she is a modern-day Ralph Nader, given her consumer-protection emphasis. That, however, is part of her problem (and that of many would-be-leaders): too much focus on singular issues. Like a tree with a single dominant image:

Source of photo unknown

Elizabeth Warren/ BPR Screengrab

Senator Chuck Schumer, by all accounts, is a very smart man. He scored a perfect 1600 on the SAT and was valedictorian of his high school class. Then Haaarvaard and all that. What is it about many really smart people that results in their being so far removed from reality? I suppose it may be because they think so far ahead and above normal people that they lose sight of what's really around them. Chuck Schumer has taken some outrageous positions on policies that may make sense to him and his supporters, but not to me. His tree is overloaded with Abilities and Authority (Branches and Trunk), while riding the backs of Republicans:

Facebook

Senator Chuck Schumer
arstechnica.com
(photo is reversed)

Senator John McCain was a true American hero who served our country in ways that are unrivaled by any other modern-day politician. He was indeed a Tree-Dimensional Leader with a beautiful balance of Authority, Abilities, and Character. He probably would have made a great president. He didn't achieve that status because, in my opinion, he was outmaneuvered by the more modern techniques employed by Barak Obama and simply by Obama's almost magical public image. John McCain was not interested in polishing his own public image; he thought his credentials alone were enough—but we should all realize by now that credentials are way down the list when it comes to America's choice for president.

That being said, Senator McCain unfortunately relegated himself to the role of a Poo Bah, and he was not particularly well-suited to that role. He miscalculated his sphere of influence when he became a "never-Trumper." His opposition to Trump during the 2016 campaign and even after the election were counterproductive and diminished McCain's own credibility. Fortunately, as President Trump's tenure in office grew, Senator McCain began to take supportive positions, but inconsistently so. McCain projected a negative persona, even when he took (rare) positive positions. (That was part of the public image problem that cost him the election.)

So a McCain tree might reflect strengths, but not in a very attractive way:

Photo by Author

Senator John McCain
Wordpress.com

A Leader Who is Neither President, Pundit, nor Poo Bah

Sometimes a leader emerges who is undeniably effective and (nearly) universally popular. I say nearly because there is ALWAYS a Pundit who cannot resist finding fault. I want to feature one such modern-day leader here at the conclusion of this chapter: **Clemson University Head Football Coach Dabo Swinney.**

Photo by Author

theoddyseyonline.com

Dabo Swinney, at the ripe old age of thirty-eight, was temporarily appointed as Clemson's head coach in October of 2008. After six games the position became permanent. In seven sometimes turbulent years, Swinney led the Clemson Tigers to the NCAA National Football Championship with a legendary play in the last second of a legendary game.

At Clemson, Coach Swinney has currently amassed an overall record of one hundred-eight wins versus thirty losses. His teams have won seven of twelve bowl games. He has under his belt one National Championship, four ACC Championships, six conference division titles, and has been named coach of the year five times. According to Darrin Donnelly in *Sports for the Soul*, "Dabo Swinney has quickly won over a nation of fans ... (with) his rags-to-riches story, his quick wit, his memorable one-liners, and his relentless confidence in the power of positive thinking ..."

Dabo is an eternally positive person who exudes authenticity, passion, optimism, humility, respect for others, enthusiasm, and a keen understanding of the importance of relationships. In other words, his Character dimension is off the scale! He loves his players, and they love him (thus the photo I chose above). And while Clemson fans have always been loyal, Dabo has advanced the culture to embrace a new "Clemson Nation."

Coach Swinney and even some of his supporters dismiss the idea that he is a genius, but the organization and culture that he has created at Clemson is nothing short of that label. For one thing, Dabo knows how to multiply his Abilities by surrounding himself with lieutenants and players who are simply the best. He creates the vision and the values, and then lets them (literally) run with it.

Chad Scott, in *Leadership Lessons You Can Learn from Clemson's Dabo Swinney* (www.nationalfootballpost.com, January 15, 2017) summarized some of Swinney's approaches:

- Keep improving.
- Surround yourself with the best lieutenants
- Surround yourself with the best "worker bees" (players).
- No ego.
- Create a culture of only the best.
- Stay positive.
- Be yourself.

Swinney's leadership strategy was described by Emily Price through an interview featured in *Upstate Business Journal* (December

19, 2014). The coach said that his strategy starts with being a "servant leader" with a genuine appreciation for each person's role. He tries to create "the right culture" and to be authentic. He has implemented amazing levels of communication, accountability, and relationships.

For example, his Director of Player Relations oversees a mind-boggling array of programs that keep him and Coach Swinney in touch with every aspect of the players lives. There is a career development program that helps prepare players for life after Clemson football. Then there is the "Swinney Huddle" that pulls together *everyone* who is not a coach but touches players in any way (academics, trainers, equipment managers, nutritionist, etc.). Also there is a group called The Council, which consists of twelve players who are selected based on their leadership skills to represent the interests, needs, and general development of all of the other players. Further, there is a Senior Leadership Group comprised of academic seniors. A really unusual program kicks off each year with a big dinner at one of the coaches' homes. At the dinner, the Senior Leadership Group conducts "The Accountability Draft," in which teams of twelve are created, and then the members of the teams are made accountable for each person on their team: following up and encouraging each other on absences, academics, even personal problems.

Focus and motivation are central to Dabo's *modus operandi*. The night before each game, for instance, the whole team watches a movie together. Then Dabo uses the concepts from the movie to motivate, inspire, and focus the team in preparation for the game.

Dabo Swinney: Authority, Ability, Character. Few can argue that this championship coach/leader demonstrates a perfect balance of the fundamentals of *Tree-Dimensional Leadership*.

I just try to lead by relationships. (Dabo Swinney)

I think from a leadership standpoint, you have to be authentic. You have to be genuine. Just be who you are. (Dabo Swinney)

You never know who's paying attention ... so whatever it is you're doing, just bloom where you're planted. (Dabo Swinney)

Let the light that shines in you be brighter than the light that shines on you. (Dabo Swinney)

We're going to do it right, and I would rather lose trying to do it right than to win knowing we didn't. (Dabo Swinney)

You can't treat everyone the same, but you have to treat everyone fair. What's fair for one isn't necessarily fair for another. (Dabo Swinney)

Coach Bear Bryant was always fair. He treated every one of us like trash. (Forrest Gump)

So there you have it: The final chapter of Tree-Dimensional Leadership, covering Presidents, Pundits, and Poo Bahs. In the process, I have most certainly alienated some readers, perhaps even pissed some off. I hope that at least I have demonstrated how the three dimensions of **Authority, Abilities, and Character**, framed among the individual properties of trees, can be used to "get your head around" the leadership qualities of those serving from the simplest to the very highest levels. In the Epilogue I will pull together the essence of the entire concept of Tree-Dimensional Leadership.

Reading the Rings

Tree-Dimensional Leadership demonstrates
that even those at the very
highest levels have access only to the same
characteristics that the rest of us do.

There is nothing magical, mystical, or
exclusive about the traits of high-level
leaders. All of them utilize varying degrees
of Authority, Abilities, and Character.

Such leaders are indeed very much like trees,
and while there is an endless variety of them,
they all have capacities and limitations just
as trees have branches, trunks, and roots.

Epilogue

> *No individual achievement can equal*
> *the pleasure of leading a group of*
> *people to achieve a worthy goal. When*
> *you cross the finish line together,*
> *there's a deep satisfaction that it*
> *was your leadership that made the*
> *difference. There's simply nothing that*
> *can compare with that.*
> *(Bill George, "Truly Authentic*
> *Leadership," USN&WR,*
> *Oct. 30, 2006)*

Now you should feel as if you have completed the initiation for an exclusive society, and you know all the secrets that provide a special understanding of Leadership. You have crossed the finish line. As mutual members of this society, we can sit back, relax, and comfortably reminisce about what Tree-Dimensional Leadership means.

We often take nature for granted. For instance, before reading this book, you may have given little thought to the basic existence and importance of the three dimensions. Hopefully, now you know a whole lot more about **Height**, **Width**, and **Depth**. This awareness alone can enrich your life. Add the concept of those three dimensions being synonymous with **Authority, Ability,** and **Character**, and you have **3-D Leadership.** Further, trees, as timeless icons of nature, embody truths and principles that are timeless. As symbols of Leadership, they can enable us to understand ourselves and others within a framework that is beautiful and just plain awesome—**Tree-Dimensional Leadership**!

Peter Wohlleben, in his charming and fascinating book *The Hidden Life of Trees* (2015), makes the powerful case that trees are social beings. He describes how trees are like human families in which parents and children live together and communicate. The parents support their youngsters, nurture those who are sick, and issue warnings of impending dangers. Wohlleben notes that trees "maintain an inner balance.... They must lengthen their branches and widen the diameter of their trunks to support their increasing weight."

In his foreword to Wohlleben's book, scientist Tim Flannery explains that trees live on a different time scale than we do. They take things on a leisurely pace. One of the oldest living trees is around 9,500 years old. Electrical impulses pass through roots of trees at the rate of one-third of an inch per second. Trees share a "wood wide web" of soil fungi that enables the sharing of an enormous amount of information. And trees share food and communicate because they need each other.

Wohlleben notes that when trees unite to create a forest, the whole is greater than its parts. I think that leaders would do well to make use of this concept, realizing that unity— certainly among followers, but also among fellow leaders—has great benefits. Root systems of the same species interconnect, resulting in exchange of nutrients and mutual support. A forest, unlike individual trees, provides mutual protection from wind, heat and cold. A tree can only be as strong as the forest that surrounds it. The average tree grows its branches out only until it encounters the branch tips of neighboring trees. In this way, trees share available air and light and avoid competition.

Support for my assertion that Character (represented by roots) is the most important dimension of leadership can be found in Wohlleben's observation that "Tree roots extend a long way, more than twice the spread of the crown." He says that roots are the most important part of a tree, and are a more decisive factor than what is growing above ground. Roots may be where the tree equivalent of a brain is located. The root looks after the survival of the tree. Roots withstand severe climatic conditions, and have actually regrown trunks over and over again. Through the root system, trees exchange information and share in numerous ways. Those are pretty good Character traits. You might consider the Character trait of Integrity as the taproot (main root) of a Tree-Dimensional Leader.

It is in the roots that centuries of experience are stored, and it is this experience that has allowed the tree's survival to the present day.
(Peter Wohlleben, in reference to a 9,550-year-old spruce in Sweden)

Young trees often spend their first few years developing their branches, which support energy-absorbing leaves or needles. During such periods, the trees appear much wider than they are tall. Compare this to the concept that potential leaders must first develop their Abilities before moving into positions of leadership and responsibility.

Wohlleben notes that after this period of branching out, especially when an old tree falls and opens up air and light, the "smartest" young trees immediately reach for the sky. Their energy is transferred now to extending the height of their trunks. Trees that dawdle get left behind, literally in the shade, and don't survive. It's easy to see the parallel with the concept of Authority as represented by height (trunks).

According to Wohlleben (p. 37):

This is what a mature, well-behaved deciduous tree looks like. It has a ramrod-straight trunk with a regular, orderly arrangement of wood fibers. The roots stretch out evenly in all directions and reach down into the earth under the tree. In its youth, the tree had narrow branches extending sideways from its trunk. They died back a long time ago, and the tree sealed them off with fresh bark and new wood so that what you see now is a long, smooth column. Only when you get to the top do you see a symmetrical crown formed of strong branches angling upward like arms raised to heaven. An ideally formed tree such as this can grow to be very old.

Photo by Author, Milliken Arboretum, Spartanburg, SC

Trees age much like we do, only much more slowly. Their bark serves many of the same purposes as our skin does, and bark wrinkles with age. The highest branches in a tree's crown get thinner with age, just as hair does with many of us. At a certain point, trees stop getting taller, so their energy is redirected to getting wider.(A couple of years ago, I realized that I had not bought any new pants in three or four years. So I went to a store and selected three or four pair in my usual size. None of them fit. All of them were one inch too long and one inch too tight in the waist. In other words, I had shrunk one inch in height and gained an inch in the waist!)

How we age, or in the case of leadership, how we meet a variety of challenges over time, can also be compared to trees that survive and thrive even in challenging environments. Wohlleben notes that "As almost no habitat on Earth offers ideal living conditions, it's actually got more to do with the tree adapting than the niche being ideal" (p.75).

Trees teach us that it is possible—desirable, perhaps even necessary—to live and thrive as part of a larger society (forests), while at the same time maintaining distinct individuality.

EPILOGUE

Photo by Author, Biltmore Estate, NC

> *To be one's self, and unafraid*
> *whether right or wrong, is*
> *more admirable than the easy*
> *cowardice of surrender to*
> *conformity.*
> *(Irving Wallace, 1916–1990,*
> *writer and screenwriter)*

In an earlier chapter, I quoted part of a beautiful poem from a Hallmark card about a stalwart oak. The second part of that poem has much to say about leadership rooted in strength:

> *The weary wind gave up and spoke,*
> *"How can you still be standing, Oak?"*
> *The oak tree said, "I know that you*
> *Can break each branch of mine in two,*
> *Carry every leaf away,*
> *Shake my limbs, and make me sway.*
> *But I have roots stretched in the earth,*
> *Growing stronger since my birth.*
> *You'll never touch them, for you see,*
> *They are the deepest part of me.*
> *Until today, I wasn't sure*
> *Of just how much I could endure.*
> *But now I've found, with thanks to you,*
> *I'm stronger than I ever knew."*

*We never know how
strong we are until
strong is the only
answer.
(Unknown)*

It has occurred to me that the greatest threat to leadership comes from within ourselves. I have made a strong case that the Nurture end of the Nature/Nurture spectrum is largely under our own control. As Tree-Dimensional leaders, we pretty much determine the proportions of our dimensions (Authority, Abilities, and Character). Too much of any dimension can interfere with our effectiveness—this is especially true of Authority and Abilities.

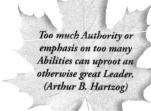

*Too much Authority or
emphasis on too many
Abilities can uproot an
otherwise great Leader.
(Arthur B. Hartzog)*

Photo by Author

Leadership is often modeled from what we observe in others. A friend of mine recently asked me to participate in a project of his gathering information about personal heroes. The following was my response, which I think deserves a place in my Epilogue about Tree-Dimensional Leadership:

I remember being impressed with the movie about Jim Thorpe's life (famous Native American athlete) that came out when I was in gram-

mar school. I was not particularly athletic at the time, but the movie inspired an interest in high-jumping, and I made my own high-jump pit, and practiced for years. When in high school, I won first place in the state high-jump competition both my junior and senior years. (As a side note, for some reason I associated the classical music composition "Hungarian Rhapsody" with that athletic pursuit; the music carries one from feelings of elation to despair and back to elation.)

My grandfather was always my hero. My father died when I was three years old, and Granddaddy was a wonderful support for my mother and me. Actually, he had numerous other grandchildren also, and he always managed to make all of us feel special. He always seemed a wise, kind and capable age of 75 years old to me, even though he was actually only 60 or so in my earliest memories. He was a farmer and operated a country store. He was respected by everyone, as he did many favors for those who needed help. Granddaddy had a great sense of humor, and he loved his family. He and Grandmama both lived to be in the mid-90s.

Younger people may seem to be more hero-prone in recent years because of movies, television and video games. While adults are also exposed to such media, young people "get into it" more. Of course children use their imaginations much more frequently and realistically than adults. I think adults have heroes also, they just don't express it as much as younger people.

Certainly heroes serve as role models. This contributes in a way to social order, because people assume roles that are needed or expected in social situations, and sometimes people may have little motivation or way to know how to behave, other than the manner in which they have observed their heroes to act.

There can also be anti-heroes. I once ran across a guy who was briefly my daughter's boss, and I did not care for him. She had changed jobs and had worked at this guy's advertising firm for only a couple of weeks, when they abruptly fired her. It was very clear that my daughter's immediate supervisor, who was a young girl with very little supervisory experience, was quite jealous of my daughter, and she made work impossible. The owner of the firm was too busy to notice or care, so he went along with firing my daughter. I paid him a visit in his posh high-rise office complex, and we got into a rather heated argument. The boss threatened to have me arrested if I did not immediately leave, and called for security. In retrospect, it was rather comical to notice the silence as everyone stopped what they were doing, and actually leaned out of doorways to see what would happen next.

I concluded by stepping into the hallway and telling the butch-haircut boss in a voice that all could hear "Never in my life have I called anyone a son of a bitch, but for you I am making an exception!" Then, of course, I made a quick exit before security arrived.

One of my good friends, Rev. Mitchell Houston, is a United Methodist minister. In an article he wrote for the May 2015 South Carolina United Methodist *Advocate* (p. 39), he related the following story about the gifts that God gives us:

An ancient legend tells of a king who walked into his garden one day to find almost everything withered and dying. Speaking to an oak near the gate, he learned that it was sick of life because it was not tall and beautiful like the pine. The pine was upset, for it could not bear delicious fruit like the pear tree, while the pear tree complained that it did not have the lovely odor of the spruce, and so it went throughout the entire garden. Coming to a pansy, the king saw its bright face full of cheerfulness.

"Well, little flower," said the monarch, "I'm glad to find at least one that is happy in this discouraging scene."

"Your majesty, I know I'm of small account, but I decided you wanted a pansy when you planted me. If you had desired an oak or a pear tree, you would have put one in my place. Therefore I've determined to be the best flower I can be!"

While it can be helpful to be *motivated* by heroes and other models, it can be very limiting to *compare* your leadership qualities, potential or accomplishments with others. The secret is to *be the best that you can be.* Assess your own qualities, potential and accomplishments. That will be quite enough to keep you on your toes. If you are an oak tree, there is no value in comparing yourself to the adjacent mimosa.

I find exact parallels to the trilogy of **Authority, Abilities, and Character** in just about every facet of life, politics, and human relationships. Let me share the following as I tie up loose ends to conclude this book:

One of my all-time favorite quotes, which I have applied over time as a sort of personal motto and used in my email signature for many years, is this (attributed to Meryl Runion, communications expert):

> *Say what you mean,*
> *Mean what you say,*
> *But don't be mean when you say it.*

The lines perfectly reflect the three Leadership Dimensions:

> *Say what you mean* (**Ability**)
> *Mean what you say* (**Authority**)
> *But don't be mean when you say it.* (**Character**)

The three branches of the federal government, for heaven's sake, clearly reflect the 3-D concept:

> *Legislative (makes laws):* **Ability**
> *Executive (enforces laws):* **Authority**
> *Judicial (judgments/values/morals):* **Character**

We often refer to "mind, body and spirit" when applying various principles. Again, a perfect fit:

> *Mind* (**Abilities**)
> *Body* (**Authority**)
> *Spirit* (**Character**)

The Holy Trinity can be seen in the same light:

> *Father* (**Authority**)
> *Son* (**Ability**)
> *Holy Spirit* (**Character**)

One final example:

> *Past* (**Character**)
> *Present* (**Authority**)
> *Future* (**Abilities**)

Now I want to share a few words about Leadership and *significance*. It doesn't take a genius to realize that effective leaders impact incalculable numbers of lives, and in ways that are often unexpected or even unknown. Like ripples in water, the actions of leaders have far-reaching effects that extend in all directions and can continue long after the act itself.

I like to consider myself a rather effective Tree-Dimensional Leader. (And I suppose that should be expected if I am to publish a book on the topic!) When I retired (the first time ☺) as dean of students at Spartanburg Methodist College, an associate who had been on my staff for a number of years wrote me a letter that deeply moved me. I am proud to share the essence of that letter below, because I think it demonstrates the significance that Tree-Dimensional Leadership can have in unexpected ways:

> *Art,*
>
> *It is hard to believe this day has arrived ... As you close your office door for the final time, please remember the impact you have had on your staff, with the students, and throughout the SMC community.*
>
> *Thank you for the times you let me talk through my concerns until I reached a solution. Your quiet presence and gentle nudges allowed me the room to grow as a professional with the security of your support.*
>
> *Thank you for supporting me when irate parents or coaches called complaining about a decision I had made.*

Thank you for standing up for the Hall Directors to create understanding within the SMC community about the work they do.

Thank you for creating a relaxed work environment. The hours alone are stressful enough but your humor and laid-back approach eased so much of the tension.

Thank you for support in my mission to obtain my master's degree.

Thank you for providing me with this opportunity and for believing in me. I recognize there are not many colleges who would have hired (someone with my degree) for the position. I am grateful you saw my passion and believed in me.

Thank you for your love, support, and prayers during my difficult times. I will always remember the love in your eyes when I told you I was pregnant (after several miscarriages). You were never 'just a boss,' you have always been a friend.

There is no way I could list all of the things I am thankful for. You have made such an impact on me and helped me develop in this profession. If anything you taught me to listen to my gut instincts.

I am so grateful I do not have to say good-bye. (Our church) has joined us and now you are stuck seeing me on Sundays. Enjoy your last day and think about us when you are lounging on your deck. I know we will think of you often.

With love,
Stacey

[I should note here that I did retire from the college for seven blissful years, but I was invited to return to "active duty" for one year as interim dean. I shamelessly suggest that such an invitation is further evidence that I did something right in the field of Leadership.]

We never know what we do in our work that will be remembered, that will be holy. It has nothing to do with our job titles. It has everything to do with the faith, vision and love that we bring to it.
(Rabbi Jeffrey K. Salkin, "Being God's Partner", 1994)

A life isn't significant except for its impact on other lives.
(Jackie Robinson)

Inspire someone today and you will inspire yourself. By spreading goodness, you gently brush immortality.
(Mimi Goss, "What is Your One Sentence?")

The image of a Tree of Life used on the cover of this book and repeated several times throughout, is the most beautiful rendition with a three-dimensional effect that I could find. It is a perfect model for Tree-Dimensional Leadership.

Tree of Life symbols have been around for centuries, portrayed in various media and for all sorts of purposes. I found this passage on a plaque in a gift shop, which explains the concept quite well.

Sacred Tree/Tree of Life
Spiritual Energy, Wisdom

The sacred tree or Tree of Life represents the fruitfulness of the earth, evoking spiritual growth, abundance, and rebirth. Rooted in the heart of the earth, it drinks the sacred waters of life and stretches its branches into the heavens, providing a bridge between celestial and earthly powers. Each Celtic tribe had its own sacred tree, a symbol of sovereignty, sacred wisdom, and spiritual energy.

Texte Francais Ci-Dessous

> *The best leaders ... almost without exception and at every level, are master users of stories and symbols.*
> *(Tom Peters, business writer)*

With the above quote in mind, I will close with the following story, which is one with deep personal meaning to my wife and me:

My special relationship with trees began fifty-three years ago. Alongside the narrow two-lane road leading to the home of the love of my life (my wife-to-be) was a pasture; atop a low hill in the middle of that pasture, framed by the sunset, I noticed the stark outline of a very old tree. It had seen its best years, but I had great respect for that tree. I imagined how it had withstood the passage of time, growing from a seedling, flourishing, maturing through seasons, storms, and heaven knows what challenges—all the while aging gracefully. Jean and I were just beginning our relationship; I told her that I hoped it would always be there for us—a reminder of our everlasting love. I gave it a name: *Halcyon*—which means *calm, peaceful or tranquil; also prosperous or carefree.* The last time we rode by the pasture just a few years ago, the tree was not visible—but that doesn't mean it's not still there. Its roots may have turned to humus, but I believe that the spirit of trees can last forever, and that even some physical parts of them can become rejuvenated in the soil, and support new forms of life that continue on. My wife and I drove by that tree many times over the years, and it became a symbol that has often resurfaced in my consciousness.

In 1965, a year after we "discovered" Halcyon, I wrote a poem to preserve its memory and to express its meaning for our lives; a few years later, I painted its image. The poem and painting follow:

After One Year Together ...
"Halcyon"

There is a tree that guards a hill we know ...
Halcyon, its name must be—
For constant Calm it seems, in sun or snow.
Tempestuous storms the world may bring ...
Our Tree remains the same.

One year has passed since first we knew ...
Our Friend for what he is—
An Ageless Sign, a Mark, that can imbue
In each of us that tender grace
Of simple, perfect love.

Yet need we prove by outward sign ...
What in our hearts we <u>know</u>—
When Halcyon, with outstretched arms, benign,
Smiles upon our virgin Love,
Our chaste and sterling bond?

One year has passed, and in that time ...
Our Friend has never changed—
Nor ever will, though up his Form may climb
The crazing lines of aging Life—
But Life which never ends.

Through autumn days we've seen him stand ...
Through winter, bleak and cold—
In sylvan spring we saw his extant hand ...
When summer came we even stood
In the shadow of his smile.

And even now, though far away ...
We know that he is there—
Our Halcyon, Eternal Friend, our Stay;
Immutable Love personified,
Life which never ends.

I want to share one more poem that I wrote during my college days that seems appropriate for the last word:

Reaching

I reached from a Dark, Shapeless World

For Something with Substance,
with Form;

But the space between
the thought and deed—
the time it took to act—

Has changed the Dark
to Light.

Or was it What I touched?

About the Author

D r. Arthur B. Hartzog is a retired college administrator who has experienced leadership in numerous settings for more than half a century. Growing up in a small town in the 1950s, he served as a leader in his church, school, and community. His father died when Art was three years old, and his mother and grandparents made many sacrifices to support him and his three older siblings. He held at least ten part-time jobs, including shoe-shine boy, newspaper delivery, picking cotton and working in his grandfather's country store, soda jerk, and lifeguard.

At the University of South Carolina, Art expanded far beyond his small-town roots, serving in numerous leadership roles. He was selected for such awards as Who's Who, Top Ten Student (of ten thousand–plus students), Outstanding Senior, membership in honor societies, and various leadership awards in his Air Force ROTC unit.

After obtaining his master's degree, Art served four years on active duty with the air force, receiving the Air Force Commendation Medal. He remained in the Air Force Reserves, garnering more awards and gaining early promotion to the rank of major.

Art worked at Clemson University, then earned his PhD at Florida State University in Higher Education Administration. He served as dean of students and vice president at Coker College, then as Executive Director of the Darlington County Community Action Agency, and finally retired as dean of students at Spartanburg Methodist College. Throughout his career, Dr. Hartzog has been active in his church. He has studied leadership and shared his expertise with students and professional organizations.

Dr. Hartzog's wife Jean is a retired elementary school teacher, and they have two children: Art, Jr and Julie. Art, Jr is a civil engineer, and his wife Kaoru is a family practice physician. Julie is a Registered Nurse, and her daughter Anna (Dr. and Mrs. Hartzog's only grandchild) is the most special part of their lives.